ON THE CREST OF THE HILL

DEVIZES
Secondary School.

Main School.

FOUNDED 1906.

On the Crest of the Hill

*Devizes Grammar School
1906 – 1969*

*compiled and introduced by
Lorna Haycock*

First published in the United Kingdom in 2006 by The Hobnob Press, PO Box 1838, East Knoyle, Salisbury SP3 6FA

© Dr Lorna Haycock and contributors 2006

All rights reserved. No part of this publication may be reproduced, stored in a retrieval system, or transmitted, in any form or by any means, electronic, mechanical, photocopying, recording or otherwise, without the prior permission of the publisher and copyright holder.

British Library Cataloguing in Publication Data
A catalogue record for this book is available from the British Library.

ISBN10 0-946418-48-9
ISBN13 (from January 2007) 978-0-946418-48-0

Typeset in 11/15 pt Scala
Typesetting and origination by John Chandler
Printed in Great Britain by Salisbury Printing Company Ltd, Salisbury

Foreword

WHAT GREATER PLEASURE than to be asked to reminisce about my time at Devizes Grammar School! I was incredibly happy there – for too short a time, given a peripatetic childhood; my father was a doctor in the Air Force. It was my first year of grammar school, though, and got me off to a flying start.

I had taken the entrance test from a girls' fee-paying prep. school in Shropshire, where, busily playing cricket and getting regular black eyes, I had been completely unprepared. The Head told my parents (with a slight look of horror on her face) that no one had ever taken the test from her school before!

Grammar School was a new experience and I took to it, especially rubbing along with boys for the first time, with the speed of a Kelly Holmes. I soon had my first boyfriend and we caught the same bus to school every morning. I had a fair way to come from RAF Upavon, and a group of us used to while away the time smoking on the upper deck. It wasn't long before concerned members of the public were reporting us! We became a lot more circumspect but still carried on, buying our packets of five Wills Woodbines from the little shop opposite the school gates. I had grown out of smoking by the age of thirteen.

Devizes Grammar School gave me such a good grounding and taught me to enjoy learning as well as boys. It was a carefree, instructive time that left me superbly well prepared for my future schools. I look back very fondly and treasure the memories.

Sandra Howard (née Paul)

Introduction

My teaching career started inauspiciously. Two days before the beginning of the Autumn term 1951 I was stricken with measles, the result perhaps of a spell of teaching practice at a primary school in my home town, Andover. After a fortnight I was well enough to come to Devizes, only to find that the school was closed for the period 8-15 October because of army manoeuvres on the Plain.

A visit to Braeside the previous summer had left me somewhat apprehensive about what I might expect. Following the death of the revered Miss Janaway earlier that year, History had been taught by temporary staff; discipline had become lax and the exam forms were ill prepared. The first year was hard; the delay in my arrival and the manoeuvres meant that precious time had been lost. As I was only a few years older than my sixth form pupils, I had to be quite firm. This was my first teaching post, so there was a lot of preparation and marking to do, particularly as I taught throughout the school, so exam time was a nightmare.

But the kindness and welcome given by senior staff and the friendly atmosphere of the school soon made me feel more relaxed, and I really enjoyed teaching my subject. I quickly realised how lucky I was to have landed a job in such a delightful school. The 'family' feel of the place, despite the physical division into two establishments, is something that recurs again and again in the reminiscences of former pupils. It was small enough to get to know everyone and follow their progress throughout the school, and I feel fortunate that I can count many of them as my friends after so many years. I am glad to have this opportunity to gather together the memories of a school which was sacrificed to political ideology, but which had such a positive effect on the lives of so many. I hope that the ensuing recollections will reflect the results of sixty- three years of 'education' in the true sense of the word– 'bringing out'.

I must express my sincere thanks to all those past pupils who have contributed reminiscences, photographs and other material to this book. I hope that the resulting volume will truly illustrate the ethos of the school and the affection in which it is held by those who were educated there.

Lorna Haycock

List of Contributors

Peter Amor
Sybil Amor (née Humphries)
Mrs Backhouse (née Chivers)
Heather Benger
Lorna Bishop (née Bush)
The late Tom Blake
Pamela Bracher (née Lye)
Pauline Bradbury (née Cox)
Mary Bradley (née Ellis)
Paulette Bremner-Milne (née Dicker)
Hugh Burn
Alan Carter
Betty Cawley (née Green)
Olive Chivers
Maisie Connor (née Brown)
Bill Crosbie-Hill
Robert Crowder
David Davis
Paul Drinkwater
Tony Duck
Joan Flint (née Davis)
Barbara Fuller (née Bobby)
Victor Gane
Terry Gaylard
Barbara George (née Jessett)
Richard Giles
John Girvan
Peter Greed
Peggy Gye (née Welch)
The late Lily Hamblin
Graham Hancock
Jean Hancock (née Ware)
Peggy Hehir (née Cleverly)
Patsy Hehir

Chris Henley
The late Lily Hinxman
Sandra Howard (née Paul)
Hilary Hunt (née Smith)
Terry Iles
David Jessett
The late Roy Kemp
Pat Kennedy
Jennifer Lake (née Burt)
John Leech
Pat Macey (née Williams)
Leonard Mills
Michael Oliver
Peter Paget
Jean Parsons (née Davis)
David Pickering
Sir Michael Pitt
Lady Maria Pitt (née Di Claudio)
Susan Queen (née Denton)
The late Vera Rendell (née Drewell)
Jim Smith
Charlie Springford
Roger Swift
Gina Tay
Diana Travers (née Bond)
Freda Vince (née Rossiter)
Donald Watts
Shelagh Way (née Newland)
Chris Wiltshire
Keith Wiltshire
Gill Winchcombe (née Huntley)
Philip Winchcombe
Margaret Worth (née Rendell)

THE SCHOOL came into being as a result of the Education Act of 1902, which made county councils remedy the deficiencies in secondary schooling and provide an educational ladder for promising boys and girls. As a proprietary Grammar School run by Mr Pugh still existed at Heathcote House on the Green, the school which started in Bath Road in 1906 was known as Devizes Secondary School.

The school was opened on 8 September by the Marquis of Bath, Chairman of Wiltshire County Council. Built by Long and Co. of Bath, with hot water heating by Hadens of Trowbridge, at a cost of £7,250, it was described in the *Devizes and Wiltshire Gazette* as ' the most up to date school in the county and in proportion to its size the most costly'. Money was raised for the construction by subscriptions, loans on the security of the Urban and Rural District Council rates and by the sale of the old British School in Northgate Street. Designed by R E Brinkworth of Bath and Chippenham, the building was constructed of Newbury orange-coloured and sandy-faced bricks and Bath stone, with green roof slates. An assembly hall 38° feet long and 26° feet wide could be extended by a partition room, giving a total length of 55° feet. The floor consisted of pitch blocks laid on concrete, and two classrooms opened off each side of the hall. A cookery room

---

CONDITIONS OF ADMISSION.
AGES FOR SCHOOL.

22. Subject to the provisions of Article 2 (*b*), no Pupil shall be admitted to the School under the age of 10 years ; but until the Governors otherwise determine the minimum age on admission shall be 11 years, except in cases recommended by the Head Master and approved by the Governors. No Pupil shall remain in the School after the end of the School year in which the age of 18 is attained except with the permission of the Governors, which in special cases may be given upon the recommendation of the Head Master, until the end of the School year in which the age of 19 is attained.

TO WHOM THE SCHOOL IS OPEN.

23. (*a*) The School shall be opened only to Day Pupils, that is to say, pupils residing with parents, guardians or near relatives, or in the house of any person approved by the Governors.

(*b*) No pupil shall be admitted to the School unless he or she is of good character, and of sufficient health, and has been found fit for admission in an examination under the direction of the Head Master, graduated according to the age of the Pupil, or as the result of some other examination approved by the Governors for the purpose. If there is not sufficient room for all Pupils so found fit, preference shall be given to those who are children of inhabitants or rate-payers within the Devizes Union.

Extract from articles - nos. 22 & 23

and manual instruction room were connected to the main building by corridors. A Headmaster's room, Assistant Mistress's room and Secretary's office completed the ground floor accommodation. Fireproof stairs led to the first floor rooms, an Art room with an easel area, a lecture room with a rising floor and a lab. with a balance room and two cupboards with sliding glass shutters, where fumes from experiments could be carried off by flues in the wall between the lecture room and the lab. Throughout the building the décor was buff walls and green paint.

The school provided space for 120 pupils. Initially there were 34 pupils and five staff – Mr Atkinson, Mr Tratman, Miss M E Jones, Miss J E Jones and Miss Watson, under the headmaster Mr E A Eden. Throughout its sixty-three year existence the school had five heads – E A Eden, E S Roberts, H F Halliwell, D W John and T C Davis.

The first admission register in 1906 lists the occupations of pupils' fathers. Apart from a Police Superintendent, a schoolmaster and a Baptist minister, the jobs fall into the group we should now call C1 – clerks, tradesmen and small farmers.

Occupations of Pupils' Fathers 1906

Baptist minister	Farm bailiff	Police Superintendent
Builder	Gardener	Porter
Butcher	Grocer	Postmaster
Clerk	Groom	Saddler
Coachman	Innkeeper	Schoolmaster
Colliery agent	Ironmonger	Signalman
Draper	Mason	Tailor
Farmer	Painter	Watchmaker

Within the next few years rising pupil numbers necessitated more accommodation. Formerly called Beltwood Dalling, Braeside was for a year the home of explorer Ernest Shackleton, c. 1913, but during the First World War was used as a convalescent home for wounded officers. The house was acquired in 1920 to provide a preparatory department, with the top floors used for the Headmaster's accommodation. As the number of pupils increased steadily, to 194 (and 48 in the prep. department) in 1930, conditions became overcrowded, His Majesty's Inspectors noting that the accommodation was 'inconvenient, inadequate and out of date'. In 1938 it was decided to close the prep. department and use the rooms in Braeside for senior classes.

Braeside as a First World War Auxiliary military hospital

By then the Headmaster had moved out to live in Long Street on his retirement in 1932. Mr Eden had led the school for twenty-six years. Selected from 140 applicants, he had come here from King Edward's Grammar School in Bath. Comments in the 1939 school magazine on the death of 'The Boss' record the wise leadership which had established the school on a firm footing:

> *To his inspiration the Devizes Secondary School owes much of its past success and its fine tradition—-*
> *Many old students —look back with gratitude and affection to his memory—-*
> *He lived for his work and the school was his life*
> *He managed to communicate to us that feeling of building something, striving for something.*

His successor, Mr Roberts, from Whitgift Grammar School, Croydon, made changes during his eleven year tenure of the post. In his address at Speech Day 1934, he said 'our principal aim — is to fit our pupils for a full life in the world'. In 1935 he hoped that 'those who pass through will have learnt how to think straight, how to find and preserve the things of this life that are worthwhile'. Two years later he continued his message – 'they must have a sense of values—a faith – a basic Christianity—if they are not to be swept away on the tide of materialism'.

Soon these values were to be tested by the outbreak of the Second World War, which not only took the lives of seventeen former pupils but also caused

E A Eden, Headmaster 1906-1932

great disruption to the running of the school. The beginning of the Autumn term 1939 was delayed by the arrival of evacuees at Braeside and the Bath Road building, which were used as reception centres. On 2 September thirty blind people and their helpers arrived unexpectedly to be billeted at Braeside for the weekend, followed soon after by parties of women and babies, and finally the Ursuline Convent from London who were to share the school for lessons, necessitating part-time attendance for both sets of pupils. The lower two Devizes forms had a day off a week, the first forms on Tuesdays and the second forms on Thursdays, attending for as little as eighteen hours, with school closing at 3 p.m. to avoid the blackout. Activities such as sports and visits were severely curtailed. Gas masks had to be carried everywhere and regular stirrup pump practices and the covering of windows with strips of gauze reminded pupils of the threat of air raids, when the Braeside cellars and the stairs in the Bath Road building became regular refuges. Some members of staff served as Air Raid Wardens and fire watching took place until 1943, with three members of staff and older boys on duty each night. Camp beds were provided and the watchers were paid three shillings a night during the summer and four shillings and sixpence in the winter.

Frequent changes of staff caused disruption. Of twenty-four members of staff appointed since 1943, only eight were still in the school in 1950. Many masters, including the Head, Mr Roberts, were called up, so older and married teachers came out of retirement to cover classes. 'Froggy' Lund became temporary Head, or as *The Gazette* unfortunately phrased it – 'Mr Lund is carrying on with married women in the absence of Mr Roberts in the RAF'. Time tabling and room allocation must have been a great challenge, with two schools sharing the buildings. Materials such as exercise books were in short supply and buses home for country pupils infrequent. Swimming lessons were cancelled as the pool was needed for the armed forces. In the Autumn pupils had to collect rose hips to provide vitamin C for babies and small children. For several years the school ran harvest camps during the summer holidays at Higher Bridmore Farm in south Wiltshire, an average of forty attending and carrying out tasks such as stooking, carting, ricking and threshing, often working ten hours a day. The school fields were ploughed up to grow vegetables and bee hives were installed. School dinners had started, with between 400 and 600 meals a week being served at 5d. a head, sometimes including nettles picked by the First Form in the Braeside woods. The school collected comforts for the Spitfire fund as well as for the troops and prisoners of war, and adopted two Merchant Navy ships – 'Bardiston' and 'British Promise', with pupils writing letters and sending parcels to the sailors.

H F Halliwell, Headmaster 1943-1951

Mr Roberts resigned in 1943 and was succeeded by H F Halliwell, chosen from 278 applicants. A man of great energy and dynamism, he steered the school through the difficult period of adjustment at the end of the war and brought new ideas and direction to school life. Activities which had been suspended during the war were restored and new ones begun – the dramatic society, athletic and swimming sports, the verse–speaking competition and the cross country. The latter became the highlight of the sporting year. Afterwards bedraggled competitors tried to wash off the mud in tin baths filled with water in the Canteen by the indefatigable 'Fuzz' Rutter; no showers in those days! A General Fund was established in 1944 to finance visits, games and music, augmented with proceeds from the summer fête. To enrich the social side of school life, a Seniors Club on Monday evenings for the Fourth, Fifth and Sixth Forms occupied pupils with quizzes, tennis and visits to the theatre, and the experiment was begun in 1946 of allocating the last one and a half hours on Friday afternoons for hobbies and creative activities, such as photography, crafts, games, dancing and music. During this period the grounds at Braeside were restored and transformed

When Halliwell was appointed to Keele University in 1951, where he was to enjoy a distinguished career as Professor in Chemical Education, the School Governors commended his 'freshness of outlook, boundless energy and enthusiasm'—his 'resourcefulness in dealing with the many problems of administration' and concluded that he had 'set a high standard— in the tone of the school'. His replacement, Denys John, took up the post in January 1952, after a brief interregnum with Harold Lewis as Acting Headmaster. Coming from a progressive co-educational boarding school, Bedales, where he had been a house master, Mr John, too, brought new ideas and a fresh approach. Even-tempered and cultured, he encouraged new activities such as the Italic Handwriting Club and the Debating Society and re-established the Parent-Teacher Association. When he left to start a new school at Nailsea in 1959, the Governors noted that the general tone of the school was better than ever.

Extra-curricular clubs and societies proliferated during the fifties and sixties – Dancing Club, Christian Union, Jazz Club, Film Society, Meteorological Club, Art Club and Recorded Music Society, despite the fact that roughly half the pupils lived in surrounding villages. Foreign, London and theatre visits, and trips to the Varsity match at Twickenham, made possible by the commitment of time and effort by staff, all helped to widen the experience and interests of students from a largely rural background.

Several long-serving members of staff retired in these two decades. 'Froggy' Lund, he of the bicycle and the Gladstone bag, who had served the school for ninety-four terms, finally left in 1950, after giving what the governors described as 'ungrudging and unstinting service'. In 1958, 'Millie' Guy, a former pupil and a member of staff for thirty years, seven of them as Senior Mistress, left a gap that was hard to fill; her Christian kindness and devotion to the school were legendary. In 1960, Olive Chivers, another former pupil and school secretary for twenty-two years, left to take up teacher training, which she had selflessly postponed in order to help the incoming avuncular Head, Tom Davis, to settle into his new role. Olive Chivers was described by a colleague as a 'perfectionist – she had devoted her life to making the school run smoothly and efficiently'. Mr Burt, who had taught woodwork from 1928, retired in 1966, the magazine that year referring to his 'father-like presence with an air of calm control and sure touch'. Harold Lewis, who in the background as

Miss Guy

Senior Master, Acting Head and time table maker had done so much to smooth the path of successive Heads, thought it right, in view of the impending amalgamation with Southbroom School, to give his successor Ron Beasley adequate time for forward planning in conjunction with the heads of the two former schools.

Plans for a new Grammar School in Southbroom Park had been afoot as early as 1928. In the county's 1946 Education Plan, provision was made for a new 2-form entry Grammar School for 320 pupils to be built between 1947 and 1949. By the Sixties the space problem had become acute. The Old Students' magazine commented in February 1959, 'It will astonish many old students who were here ten or twenty years ago— that exactly the same accommodation as they knew is now catering for three pupils where there used to be two'. There were classes of thirty-one in the science labs and girls' gym classes sometimes numbered forty. Inspectors in 1962 noted that pupils and staff were working cheerfully in difficult conditions. Braeside's internal layout, lighting, sanitary facilities and heating were woefully inadequate. The school had no proper gymnasium or playing fields of its own. Sometimes both the main school and the Braeside staff rooms had standing room only. By 1966, as pupil numbers passed the 400 mark, every possible teaching space had been pressed into use. By now the Governors were fully aware of the danger to pupils crossing the Bath Road from the increasingly heavy traffic, so pressure was exerted to expedite the new building. Detailed plans for a four–storey Grammar School were approved by the Ministry of Education in 1964, with a two and a half form entry, 465 places and a sixth form of 90. But by 1966 the political climate had changed and the Borough and District Councils gave qualified approval to the establishment of a comprehensive school at Southbroom.

So passed into history a sound school with a good relationship between staff and pupils, an increasingly impressive academic record and the education of well-rounded individuals. Successive inspectors commented on the 'happy atmosphere' and 'sound, conscientious and good work', 'noticeably good behaviour and the courtesy of boys and girls'. That the school included pupils from disadvantaged backgrounds is evidenced by the institution of free meals and clothing allowances in the 1960s. DGS was very much 'a family school', with generations of the same family attending, the Axfords, Hockleys, Mintys and Portches being prime examples. The Paget family in particular had twenty five members in the school for the whole of its existence. Colin Paget, unhappily killed in the First World War, was one of the first pupils in 1906. Former scholars who have achieved success and fulfilment in many different walks of life can perhaps identify with an old boy writing in the 1965 magazine – 'an overall memory, of eight full years, is one of happiness, tinged with regret that time has passed so quickly'.

Chronology

1906	Opening of Devizes Secondary School by the Marquis of Bath
1907	1st annual prize giving at the School
1908	Appointment of Miss Float as Senior Mistress
1909	Foundation of the Old Students' Association
1910	1st School magazine
1911	1st General Inspection
1916	1st girls admitted to houses
1918	Appointment of Miss Paradise and Miss Fisher
1919	Appointment of Mr Lund
1920	Opening of the preparatory department at Braeside
1921	Appointment of Mr Jones
	Mr Lund became Senior Master
	Unveiling of memorial to Old Boys who died in World War I
1922	General Inspection
1923	House Challenge Cup for athletic sports presented by Old Students' Association.
1924	School trip to Wembley exhibition
1928	Appointment of Miss Guy, Mr Burt and Mr Howells
1930	Summer uniform for girls introduced
	Retirement of Miss Float and appointment of Miss Fudge as Senior Mistress.
	General Inspection
1931	Appointment of Mr Lewis
1932	Retirement of Mr Eden and Miss Fisher
	Appointment of Mr E S Roberts as Headmaster
	1st prize giving in the Town Hall
1933	Lodge made available for prefects
	Parents' Association formed
1934	Introduction of 2 periods of games a week in school time
1935	1st annual school trip to London
	1st trip abroad – to Belgium
	Formation of Dramatic Society
1938	1st Old Students reunion at the Castle Hotel

Closure of prep. department
St Patrick's house formed
1st carol party
1st concert to be held in the Town Hall
Death of Mr Eden

1939 *School used as reception centre for evacuees*
1940 *School dinners started*
School shared with Ursuline Convent from Ilford
Mr Lund became Acting Headmaster
Eden Memorial Prize for Science
1941 *Parents' Association discontinued*
Resignation of Miss Fudge; replacement as Senior Mistress by Miss Buchan-Sydeserff
1942 *Ursuline Convent School returned to Ilford*
Fire watching at Bath Road building
1st Harvest Camp
1943 *Resignation of Mr Roberts and appointment of Mr Halliwell as Headmaster*
Retirement of Miss Paradise.
1944 *Prize giving ceremony revived; held in the Town Hall*
Name officially changed to Devizes Grammar School though not in use till 1946. Appointment of Mr Gobat.
1945 *Canteen built at Braeside and fitted out as a theatre and concert hall*
Dramatic Society re-formed
Verse speaking competition begun
Abolition of fees under the 1944 Education Act
1946 *Resignation of Miss Buchan-Sydeserff and appointment of Miss Janaway as Senior Mistress*
General Inspection
1947 *Deaths of Mr W G Jones and Sergeant Hiscock*
Brass plaque commemorating 17 Old Boys who died in World War II
Braeside grounds laid out
1948 *Prize giving held in the Palace Cinema. School magazine re-started.*
1949 *Prize giving held in the Regal Cinema*
Award of Plunkett-Greene Memorial Prize to school choir for best performance in the Wiltshire Music Festival
Extension of Domestic Science and Woodwork rooms and provision of a sick room
Swimming Gala organised

1950	*Retirement of Mr Lund*
	Beginning of sex education
	School Cricket XI won the Wiltshire Grammar Schools Cricket Cup
1951	*Death of Miss Janaway. Appointment of Miss Guy as Senior Mistress*
	School trip to Festival of Britain
	Resignation of Mr Halliwell and appointment of Mr John as Headmaster
	General Certificate of Education replaced School Certificate
	School closed for army manoeuvres (October)
1952	*Death of Mr Gobat*
	St Patrick's house disbanded
	Mr T E Watkins in charge of Junior School
	1st prize giving held in the Corn Exchange
1953	*Construction of Open Air Theatre*
	School party visited Paris
	1st Old Students' reunion since the war held at The Castle Hotel
1954	*Parent-Teacher Association re-formed*
1955	*School choir won the Plunkett-Greene award for best choral performance at The Wiltshire Music Festival and the School Quartet won the Weeks Memorial Shield for the best instrumental performance*
1956	*Golden Jubilee celebrations*
1957	*Presentation of gates to Braeside by the Old Students' Association*
1958	*Retirement of Miss Guy*
1959	*Resignation of Mr John as Headmaster and replacement by Mr Davis*
1960	*General Inspection*
	Resignation of Miss Chivers as School Secretary
1964	*Introduction of Spanish into the curriculum*
1966	*Retirement of Mr Burt*
1967	*Retirement of Mr Lewis*
1968	*Free meals introduced for needy students*
1969	*Closure of the school*

'Those who have left are not perished as though they had never been. Everything people do at school, good, bad and funny, leaves its mark somewhere in the life of the school'.

Denys John, writing in the Old Students' magazine, February 1958.

Reminiscences by Some of the First Pupils

Making a good name for the school

How exciting those first few days were and how proud we were to be scholars at such a lovely school. The rooms were large and lofty, with big windows, and everything was impressively clean. For most of the pupils it was their first experience of a mixed school and they were taught by two masters and two mistresses, who wore caps and gowns at all lessons.

The first day passed very quickly and not much work was done but we soon found we had to settle down and work really hard. The discipline was very strict, indeed not only in school but outside also, for we were always being told the school must make a good name for itself. The fact that detention was given if more than two pupils walked abreast on the pavement is a good example. The ground at the back of the school seemed quite large and the fives courts were always in use after school hours.

Another thing which seemed strange was that a full-time caretaker was always at hand and many times we went to him in those days for help and we always received it. For most, when the time came to leave, it was a very sad farewell.

The late Lily Hamblin (1906- ?)

The Boss

How important it all seemed – the hall (so vast), the Sergeant, the Boss's mortar board——every lesson an adventure.

One Saturday morning, led by the Boss in the famous Norfolk jacket and cycling breeches he reserved for sporting occasions, we were given our first lesson in hockey. When winter came we trundled behind a horse to far-away Chippenham where, after our usual defeat at hockey, we enjoyed tea and games and an exciting glimpse of a slightly older school.

And the first swimming lessons! Well covered in bathing dresses and with every concession to decorum by the local dressmaker, we found courage to enter the water, and the old canal enclosure became our private heaven.

How well the Boss knew how to inspire effort! Given most varied material, he shaped us into a community. It was his achievement to teach us to share alike in good fortune and bad, and we grew acutely conscious of Devizes Secondary School as something alive and growing.

The late Lily Hinxman (1906-1909)

The above two pupils started with the school in 1906

Some Reminiscences from Pre-War Days

Hard times

My mother got a scholarship from Southbroom School to the Grammar School in 1913. Times were hard and she didn't have a school uniform. Instead she wore a hand-me-down dress with leg o'mutton sleeves and a boy's coat which buttoned up the wrong way. She had to cross a muddy field to get from Cherry Orchard to Hartmoor Road. Sometimes detention meant her getting home late, but then she had to fetch the milk from Broadleas, so there wasn't much time for homework. Often she tried to do it when walking to school, which was not very successful.

During the First World War Braeside was a hospital for war wounded and the patients would stand on the bank to watch the students go by. One day a plane came down behind Braeside so the pupils went to see it.

Heather Benger

Square bashing and a turnip

AT THE AGE OF NINE I gained a scholarship from St Peter's School and joined the prep. department of the Secondary School. When I got to the big school, there was a lot of homework, at least one and a half hours, though we often swapped homework at school. My parents were very strict and insisted I did my homework first before anything else.

P E consisted largely of square bashing under Sergeant Hiscock, who always inspected our boots and hands. I was a keen cricket fan from an early age and we used to practise against a wall of the Bath Road building, chalking three marks for stumps to bowl at. The instructor at the old swimming pool on the canal was Harry Wiltshire. He tied a rope round your middle, then made you jump off the springboard and start swimming.

I remember under Mr Lewry we grew a monster turnip, weighing 14 lbs., which was taken to a fruit shop in the Market Place

After the Second World War I became secretary of the Old Students' Association, and I took part in the choruses for *Merrie England* and *The Mikado*.

Charlie Springford (1916-1919)

Let there be light!

I REMEMBER a cricket match in early June, not because of great achievements, but because on that morning news of the Battle of Jutland came through, the only decisive naval battle of the war. But there was another excitement, when the horses drawing the brake which was to take us to Marlborough Grammar School for the match bolted at the start of the journey, and we found ourselves cheered by wounded Australian soldiers as we careered up the drive to Braeside, then a military hospital for convalescents. The winter term recalls memories of bubbling gas light and the chill of the garden where the Fourth and Fifth Forms tilled the soil once a week. But a certain autumn afternoon was fully lit up when some potassium, brought down to be buried, was thrown into the canal instead, in case it still had some life in it. It had! Its incandescence was matched only by 'The Boss', who perceived this marine activity from afar and came down to investigate!

The late Roy Kemp (1910- ?)

Those cloche hats

I STARTED at Devizes Secondary School in 1916. As I then lived in Avon Road, it wasn't too far to walk. My mother, who was a seamstress, made my uniform. The outfit consisted of a navy gym tunic with a white blouse, and we wore strange shaped cloche hats in winter and panamas in summer.

I remember some of my teachers vividly. Mr Lund, who took us for French, was a tall, bespectacled figure. Miss Paradise, who taught Geography and Singing, was a dragon, who seemed to take delight in showing you up.

We learnt basic cookery, a useful skill to acquire. My favourite subjects were games and art. We played hockey matches against other schools such as Marlborough, Melksham and Trowbridge, travelling to away games by omnibus. We played games on the field backing on to the canal. In Art lessons I drew a hand, for which I received five marks out of five – I still have the picture. Being interested in Art I later went to work in Wiltshire's art shop on the corner of Maryport Street and Sidmouth Street.

Discipline at the school was strict and any transgressions were punished by detention. Mr Eden was a firm, good headmaster. The atmosphere was one of order and obedience. Millie Guy and Roy Kemp were pupils in my time. I have great memories of the school which gave me a good grounding in a very happy atmosphere.

The late Vera Rendell (née Drewell 1916-1921)

Leeches and snails

I STARTED at the Secondary School in 1922, aged 10, having passed the scholarship exam. The school at that time numbered about 250 pupils, including about 50 in the prep. department at Braeside. Class sizes were about

DEVIZES GRAMMAR SCHOOL 1906 – 1969

Girls' gym slips 1925-1926. Among the group are: G Richards, I Hockley, M Hibberd, D Edmonds, S Bachelor

DSS hockey team in the early 1920s. Back row, 3rd from left: Louise Minty; Middle row, 4th from left: Alice Powney; 2nd from right: Theresa Amor; Front row, 1st left: Emily Gregory

thirty. Mr Eden, who lived in part of Braeside, was a strict but kindly man. In 1924 I went with a group of friends to the Empire exhibition at Wembley. We didn't get home till 2 o'clock in the morning but we came to school next day, even though Mr Eden didn't expect us to attend.

Uniform, gym tunic and blouse with a girdle in your house colours, and a blazer with the DSS badge, was not strictly enforced as many parents could not afford the expense. Some pupils cycled to school while others boarded during the week in town. Village pupils brought sandwiches for lunch; the rest went home, keeping a close eye on the window of Burn's the jewellers in the Market Place, where strict Greenwich Mean Time was displayed. On wet lunch times, country dancing was sometimes held in the hall. Here, too, house parties took place at Christmas, when captains of other houses were also invited. During the weeks before, staff held dancing practices to prepare us for the event. Much effort was put into making our dresses for the party – what would Miss Float say to long *sleeveless* dresses? I remember wearing a deep rose velvet dress with beads on the waist band and a white bow in my hair.

Ronald Ponting (right) in his prefect's cap c.1924

We studied Maths and English, History and Geography, Chemistry, Physics and Botany, Cookery and Needlework. We shared the kitchen with the girls at St Peter's School. I remember making stew, rice pudding and scones. Once we each had to bring a snail in a jar for Biology. As the weekend approached, we put them in our lockers, but forgot to close the lids. By Monday morning the room was full of snails and we had to collect them up.

Physiology consisted largely of anatomy; there was no sex education, but I don't remember there being any teenage pregnancies. Smoking, however, took place in the woods. Swimming lessons in the canal pound were not very pleasant, as one encountered leeches and little fishes but the boys enjoyed their races and water sports.

Although we had detention and the occasional caning, it was a happy school and I have fond memories of my schooldays.

Jessie Backhouse (née Chivers 1922- ?)

A clip round the ear

I ENTERED THE SCHOOL on a scholarship from Bromham Council School in September 1928. The Headmaster Mr Eden was strict, capable and possessed the doubtful virtue of going 'white with anger', though not with me personally. I was far from being the only pupil to welcome his successor, Mr Roberts who at once showed that he was an admirable gentleman and a splendid administrator.

Mr Jones taught Chemistry. He had suffered greatly in the Great War, losing a leg and being very shell-shocked. He was a likeable man who took great interest in the sports, inter-school football matches, school plays and house parties. A truly dedicated encourager and supporter, he acted as starter for races. He wore a bowler hat and this headgear suited him. 'Jolly' Jones would have been a good nickname, though I must confess I never heard it used. He once chased me up the steps to the Lecture Room because I had put a waste paper basket over my head after he had given me permission to sharpen my pencil. His threats were a slight departure from the King's English and the noise of his wooden leg clumping up the stairs caused some hilarity among the class.

Mr Burt, Woodwork master, came from Newfoundland and was another likeable teacher. A fatherly figure, he strode in a stiff manner with something of a swagger. One afternoon in the Panel Room off the main hall when we were between lessons, Mr Burt arrived to discover considerable clatter and unruliness. He exclaimed in an unusually raised voice, 'If you don't stop talking, somebody will be getting hurt'. . I foolishly felt like taking him down a

1st XI football results 1928-1929 season

peg and piped up, 'Better fetch the ambulance then Sir'. This produced a most unfamiliar change in 'Uncle' Burt's countenance. He strode over to my desk and I felt the full force of an accurately aimed blow from his (glove size 11) hand on my left ear. As the blow descended he shouted, 'What's more, if I get any more of this, I'll send you to the Head'. The resultant headache lasted for the rest of the afternoon and it is not surprising that I was never saucy to Mr Burt again. But the rest of the class enjoyed the show.

After I left school in 1933, I was apprenticed to the tailors and outfitters, Clappen's, and enjoyed a long career in the retail trade. I pay tribute to the school which encouraged good citizenship and provided sound teaching of many useful subjects We were well equipped to make our way in the world wherever this would lead.

Donald Watts (1928-33)

Donald Drinkwater's School Certificate 1929

This other eden, this demi-paradise

I STARTED at Devizes Secondary School in 1928, a term after everyone else because I had come thirteenth in the scholarship examination and there were only twelve scholarships awarded. The candidates spent a day at the school, we took tests and had an interview with Mr Eden. My father, Levi Cleverly, thought that the Headmaster had discriminated against me and made a fuss, so I got a place, though I did not really want it. It was hard for my mother to afford the uniform and I hated wearing second hand gym slips with pleats that did not stay

Boys' PE in the Assembly Hall

in. Summer uniform was a salmon pink dress made from cotton bought from Kemps in the Brittox. This was good for me because my mother was a very good needlewoman. Most of the children had their fees paid by their parents and many of them came from the prep. department on the ground floor at Braeside.

My first friends were Dora Morris and Evelyn Ferris. My friend Betty Pullin who lived in the Brittox walked to school with me for the last year or so. Once she got into trouble for walking to school with her brother as boys and girls were not allowed to mix; there had been some sort of scandal a few years before. We all had to sit separately in lessons and our playgrounds were different.

In my last year at school I had to choose between a commercial course and domestic science, taught by a nice young teacher, Miss Tiddy, who later became Mrs Watkins. Every Friday I had to cook lunch for the teachers in the lodge at the end of the Braeside drive. I liked this and sometimes had to go into town to shop for the food.

Miss Fudge was the Senior Mistress and she taught games. She was very ladylike and made sure that we served underarm in tennis and bowled underarm in cricket in case we got over developed on one side. I was fairly good at sport and was in the house teams, except for swimming, as I hated the canal.

For Miss Paradise I had to write a hundred lines from my copy book, and I chose 'This other eden, this demi-paradise'. The teachers never looked at the lines, otherwise I would have got into trouble! Once Mr Bray set me a page of

The small playing field at Braeside

French to be learnt by heart. They were the only teachers to put me in detention. Only once was a boy caned – this was in assembly one Thursday morning.

Peggy Hehir (née Cleverly 1928-1934)

We felt like a family

IN SEPTEMBER 1929 came the great day when the Autumn term began. We found ourselves lined up in the Hall, boys on one side, girls on the other, waiting for our first morning assembly. Mr Eden came out of his room wearing a shabby gown and walked down the central gangway to a little reading desk in front. This first assembly was awe-inspiring. The hymn was 'Immortal, Invisible, God only wise'. I never sing that hymn without capturing the thrill I experienced then, standing in the Hall, surrounded by the honours boards. Our form room was the partition room at the end of the hall, with rows of heavy single desks with room for your books inside. Our form mistress, Miss Paradise, had a reputation for being very fierce. She issued a ruler, a pair of compasses, set-square and protractor to each of us, with the warning that we would have to replace them at our cost if we lost them. Homework started at the end of the first week. The first English homework was to read a chapter of *The Talisman*, which was our reader for that term. We had weekly form positions, which were read out at Monday morning's assembly, with Mr Eden adding caustic comments or words of encouragement. At least he knew how all his pupils were doing – there were, I believe, about 240 in the school then and we felt like a family.

Thursday was detention day, when we had a four o'clock assembly and the names were read out of those who were in detention that week for unsatisfactory work or conduct. They had to stay for about three quarters of an hour to do extra work under staff supervision in the classroom under the clock. Country children who missed their buses had to make their way home as best they could. Good work was awarded honours marks, which brought points to your house and were recorded on one's reports each term , sent by post. After collecting ten honours marks, you were eligible to try for an enamel proficiency badge, for example blue for Maths and green for Art, with the school crest in gilt. This could be achieved by 'badge work', a special piece of work arranged with the member of staff responsible for that subject. Exams were held in Maths and English at half term. Those who obtained 50% or more in both papers were allowed an extra afternoon off at the beginning of the half term break. Full exams were held at the end of every term, and, to guard against copying, classes were mixed up, with each class taking different papers.

In the autumn term came Armistice Day on 11 November, when we all met in the hall wearing our poppies, to keep the two minutes silence and to listen to the list of the Old Boys killed in the Great War. The silence was awesome and seemed to go on a long time. Just before Christmas came the evening house parties when we provided the refreshments and entertainment ourselves. There was also dancing, avoided by the boys who congregated near the door to the boys' cloakroom so that they could beat a hasty retreat if it looked as though they might have to join in. Out of class activities included nature walks on Saturday mornings, organised by Natural History master Mr Bray ('Neddy') and craft classes run by Miss Fisher on Mondays after school or sketching trips around Braeside.

Just before the end of the Spring term, it was decided that girls should have a summer uniform which could be worn instead of our serge gym tunics. The dresses were a sort of sandy-brick colour, exceedingly unbecoming when one became hot. They were complicated to make and difficult to press, with box pleats, white collars and cuffs. With these dresses we wore beige lisle stockings instead of our black woollen ones. We didn't change for PE but Miss Paradise did, sporting a gym tunic with a velvet yoke.

Miss Paradise also took us for Geography and singing. I remember little of what we did in Geography, except learn to spell 'Arctic' and 'Mediterranean'. In the first year we had to make models to illustrate life in different parts of the world, such as Japan, the Arctic and desert life. For the Arctic we used flour, salt or cotton wool, while eskimoes and polar bears were made from Christmas decorations and fragments of glass representing ice. Dad made me a plaster of paris igloo, which Miss Paradise regarded with the utmost suspicion. 'Curly' King, who had brought an offering made from cotton wool and flour all the way from Bromham on his bicycle, was disgusted with the mark he was given and dabbed some cotton wool on the floor and proceeded to powder his face. Miss Paradise put him into detention!

Sports Day during the summer term was an afternoon event held on the sports field at Nursteed Road. On one occasion we were delighted to watch a staff race. I clearly remember Mr Eden pounding down the track as though his life depended on it and Miss Fudge tripping along, taking very short steps, with her skirt billowing up over her knees in a way that was quite shocking in those days. Hockey was played in the long grass on the field behind Braeside or the grass patch at the back of the Bath Road building, where we also played cricket. Tennis was played on the grass court at Braeside.

We had 'Froggy' Lund for French and our noses were unremittingly applied to the grindstone of *Heath's French Grammar*, a deadly dull textbook. Mr Jones, who took us for Chemistry, was Welsh and temperamental. Because of his wooden leg, when he went upstairs to the lab., he was invariably followed by boys walking with a stiff leg. The most traumatic experience was having Mr Eden for Maths. We were all scared of him, though he was an excellent teacher and Maths really came alive for me. At the beginning of one autumn term, Mr Lewis, whom we called 'Alleluja', arrived to teach us Maths. In the third year we began cookery and laundry work, which was a light relief from serious studies and we did not exert ourselves greatly. Our first excursion into the realm of *haute cuisine* was to make some aptly named rock cakes. We learnt how to blue and starch, boil and dye and how to iron.

Church of England Scripture lessons were given by Canon Phipps of St Peter's and Mr Pugh, with attendance at St Peter's church once a week. Our behaviour was atrocious! Canon Phipps tried to silence us by ringing a bell, whereupon Bob Paget shouted, 'Come in!' Ours was a noisy and lively class. We also played a game between lessons. As staff teaching us frequently had to come over from Main School, there were sometimes long gaps between lessons. One game involved getting as far from the classroom and back again before the next member of staff arrived. Chemistry lessons were enlivened by water battles and chases round the lab. whenever Mr Jones's back was turned, while in Miss Fisher's lessons the boys threw sweets at each other.

In his retirement speech in 1932, Mr Eden gave us a motto – DSS – Do Some Service. At that ceremony we sang the school song and 'For he's a jolly good fellow'. Our new Headmaster, Mr Roberts, soon made changes. He disapproved of streaming, so in the fourth year we were mixed up. He gave the prefects more responsibility, making them take detention or deputise for absent staff. We now were based in B4 at the top of the stairs, formerly Mr Eden's drawing room. We had a choice of subjects – Latin or Geography, Botany and Zoology or Physics and Chemistry. For me it was a simple choice of Mr Howells or Miss Paradise. Mr Howells won hands down! Miss Guy introduced a Book Reading Scheme; we were expected, in addition to homework, to read six set books and another four chosen from a list, and then summarise them.

During my school life we had very little in the way of out of school excursions. I remember a trip by train to Fry's chocolate factory near Bristol with Miss Paradise (which added nothing to our enjoyment), visits to the magistrates' court, St John's church and the Town Hall and a trip by bus to a mediaeval fair at Lacock Abbey.

At the beginning of the summer term 1933 I handed in my term's notice required by the regulations, as my parents wanted me to leave and get a job. Inexorably the last morning came (we broke up at mid-day then); my main object was to get through without bursting into tears. The hymn that morning was 'Oh God, our help in ages past, our hope for years to come', my hope confining itself to another year with my friends at school. After a final house meeting after break, Miss Paradise said farewell to all of us who were leaving and shook hands with us, as nice as could be.

I was sad to leave, but five years later I returned as school secretary; ten years later I obtained my School Certificate and twenty-seven years later I went to college to train as a teacher

Olive Chivers (1929-1933)

The Anti-Teacher League 1933. Left to right: Olive Chivers, Mary Waight, Kitty Bolwell

Tobacco pipes and a new broom

SINCE THE AGE OF FIVE I was a pupil in the prep. department at Braeside. It was certainly not academic prowess so much as parental pressure that caused me to sit and scrape through the County exam at the age of ten. Although it was denied, there was a marked difference between the A forms and the less academic B forms, to which I was allocated from Form 1 to Form 5. After I failed the Oxford School Certificate, they moved me sideways into 5A to have another go, which was more successful.

When Mr Eden retired in 1932, Miss Fudge made a farewell presentation of an armchair which rather strangely had a pocket in one of the arms to contain tobacco pipes. She asked him in return to give the school a framed photograph of himself and this hung in the school hall at least for the remainder of my time there.

Mr Roberts was a new broom, determined to make changes, not all of which were popular. First, our uniform was altered. Until then our navy blue caps and the girls' hats had the Devizes borough arms on the front. This was changed to a DSS monogram in red, and in the case of the boys' caps, a red ring with a halo on the top. We felt this was a rather unnecessary break with tradition. Another alteration, a year or so later, was the abolition of house marks. These used to be recorded in a book kept on the window ledge in the hall and if a teacher felt that a pupil had done something particularly brilliant he would be asked to fetch the honours mark book where it would not only be recorded but all the class would know. These all counted towards your house points. The proficiency badges were also abolished. The antithesis of honour marks was detention! This took place on Thursday for an hour after school and the names in the detention book were read out by the Head at final assembly for everyone to hear. Worse still – your parents knew because of your late arrival home.

Caretakers deserve a special mention. Both Bill Bridewell at Braeside and Tom Nicholas at the main school were friendly and co-operative, serving throughout my time at the school. Bill lived 'over the shop' at Braeside after Mr Eden vacated the flat.

I look back on my schooldays with an affection I didn't feel at the time and wish I had paid more attention to the things which I now see to be interesting and valuable. Perhaps I am not alone in this.

Hugh Burn (1931-7)

Power in the workshop and the trip to London

I AM SURE we were better behaved in the thirties than are later generations. We accepted discipline from our parents and naturally did not question authority at the school and the teachers. The usual punishment for wrong doing was the writing of lines and being kept in detention. I was not aware of any pupil being expelled.

Wood and metal work were extremely popular and we often stayed at school to complete a project. Mr Burt also conducted evening classes which were well attended by adults. In my early days, no power tools were available, the wood and metal lathes being treadle operated. Suddenly over the holidays there

---

Devizes County Secondary School.

PUPIL'S REPORT BOOK.

1.—The Pupil is responsible for the care of this book when it is in his or her possession. It should not be folded but must be kept flat. If the book is lost or damaged during this time the pupil will be required to purchase another.

2.—Reports will be made at the end of each Term, *viz.*, Christmas, Easter and Midsummer.

3.—The Report Book, after the completion of each Report, should be shown to the Parent or Guardian and, after being signed, should be returned to the Headmaster.

4.—This book will be given to the pupil on leaving School as a permanent record of his or her School career.

appeared in the wood store a massive gas engine. This had apparently driven bread-making machinery at the Co-op in Northgate Street. When it became redundant it was acquired by Mr Burt plus all the shafting, lathes, drills, grinders and circular and band saws. I was most proud to be allowed to start the engine, first by lighting the gas burner on the side of the cylinder which, when red hot, fired the apparatus. It then took a great deal of effort to turn the huge fly wheel with the starting handle.

After we had completed the two year set course in wood and metal work, we were able to design and make items of our own choice. I recall making lamp standards, bookcases and a brass cannon modelled on an *HMS Victory* gun. A far bigger project was a punt, some eleven feet long and four feet wide which we launched on the canal under the supervision of Mr Burt, who took the tiller and called the stroke to the boy paddlers. Tommy Butcher, whose uncle owned Baldham Mill at Seend, obtained permission to keep the boat there, where it was often visited by parties of boys and girls over many years.

We were fortunate to enjoy many treats such as the annual visit to London, which for many of us was our first glimpse of the big city. On arrival by train at Paddington, we were met by double-decker buses to take the various groups to their places of choice, such as Westminster Abbey, a boat trip on the Thames or different museums. We met up for lunch at a Lyons Corner House, again a wonderful experience, with waitress service, music and a three course lunch. We arrived back in Devizes at 8.30, after an experience to remember for a long time. Christmas parties in the hall were also much anticipated, with dancing and games. The end of year party was usually arranged by the form teacher, and took place in the country, for example at Rosie Paget's house at Netherstreet, Old Park Farm or Baldham Mill. We usually took our tea and played rounders and handball. An annual orchestral concert took place in the hall at which various choral works were also performed. I remember giving a violin solo accompanied by Molly Gerrish, which was well received.

The distance of the Nursteed Road sports ground was a huge handicap. How did we manage without toilet facilities in the pavilion? The cross country run was never very popular. It started in the playing field, continued through Stert village, to Monument Hill and Jump Farm. Sports day was an annual event in April. Mr Lund, who was starter, took his job very seriously, while the main organiser, Mr Howells, got the older boys to help prepare the field.

During the war, while serving with the Royal Wiltshire Yeomanry in the desert I was taken prisoner. While I was incarcerated in Italy and Germany I was most grateful to receive parcels of books and cigarettes from the school and the

Old Students' Association. On my return, after an absence of five and a half years, Miss Paradise, who lived in retirement in The Breach, took me under her wing as part of my rehabilitation. She got me to undertake various manual jobs, one of which was to paint her bath. This I did, but omitted to tell her that the paint was not quite dry with the result that she took a bath and became stuck! However she treated it all as a great joke.

In the late 1960s, because of space shortages, temporary huts were erected in the grounds of Browfort. My daughter Barbara spent her lower sixth there before moving to the comprehensive school. This was a most traumatic time for pupils and parents.

David Jessett (1932-1937)

Bikes and Burners

CYCLING TO SCHOOL from Bromham was good exercise, except when I was a bit late. Dunkirk Hill seemed to get steeper the later I was and with every window of the Police Barracks looking down on me, it was a bit daunting.

Devizes Secondary School, Form IA, Summer 1933. Back row (left to right): Ruth Hibberd, Gladys Jones, Patricia Alcock, Iris Burgess, Dorothy Boulter; Middle row: Peter Godden, Roger Wellstead, Gilbert Gascoigne, Thomas Hill, Edgar Hain, Raymond Beavis, (Legger) Budd, Leonard King, Kenneth Palmer, Paul Opperman; Front row: Thomas Dewsnap, Fred Palmer, Marion Young, Mary Child, – Rogers?, Brenda Mead, Katherine Pickering, Peter Goodman, Leonard Mills

Even when I had turned the corner it was not possible to get on my bike again and those steps at the back of Shane's Castle presented a problem when I was in a hurry. Across the road and into the gateway and on around the back of the Woodwork Room to the cycle shed – phew!

In 1942, as I was cycling back from leave from the RAF, I called at a chemist's shop in Kemble, only to find myself served by Gilbert Gascogne, a fellow pupil in the class of 1932. At school he had been something of a rebel, especially in the Chemistry lab. where he delighted in pranks with the equipment there. Two of these come to mind. He would attach a rubber pipe to a gas tap on the back bench and when Mr Jones was conducting an experiment on his front bench he would blow as hard as possible into that pipe with the tap turned on and off quickly, so that there was a certain amount of air in the system. After a while Mr Jones's Bunsen burner would go out and there would be shouts from around the room to draw his attention to the fact. Another distraction would be the shooting of air gun pellets from a catapult along the rows of glass jars and containers.

I recall the song which was all the rage in 1935 – 'Dancing Cheek to Cheek' When a picture of two frogs dancing cheek to cheek appeared on the blackboard in the Art Room at Braeside, the Art Mistress did not have to look far to find the culprit. Only one girl could draw like that – Pat Alcock. Miss Moore simply said, 'Come on Pat, you can rub this off the board'.

Leonard Mills (1932-1938)

Teacher rules, O.K.?

DEVIZES SECONDARY SCHOOL provided a high standard of education and its dedicated staff had the gift of being able to strike the right balance between discipline and a friendly approach. When I started, there was no school milk in the mid-morning break, so my mother went to see Mr Roberts and after a lengthy discussion on its health properties, mother persuaded him to introduce it. We used to go to the Domestic Science kitchen to get our bottles as well as biscuits which were on sale there, probably undoing all the good the milk was providing.

Teachers had nicknames. Mr Howells was either Howler or Eggy, from his first two initials. Mr Marshall, who later sadly died on a school trip to Switzerland, was called Fritz. There was one teacher whom we mercilessly played up – Mr Jones; we didn't know at the time how cruel we were. On one of his absences we had another teacher who was strict to the extreme, and when a friend and I were caught talking we had to stay behind after school and wash out all the glass lab. equipment. One test tube contained acid which I spilt down my dress. It burnt holes all the way down, ruining my dress, socks and sandals. Then came the embarrassment of walking one and a half miles home with my uniform in tatters. As a result the teacher got a severe rebuke from the Head.

Both my brother and my eldest and youngest sons went to the Grammar School and I can't praise the high standard of education enough, which enabled them to achieve great success in their respective careers. Mr Lewis's maths teaching in particular deserves special mention. At the Grammar School there was an atmosphere not to be found in a large school, where teachers cannot have the same relationship with pupils. Miss Guy was anxious to see us develop as whole persons so she started a Scripture Union and made it appealing by holding social evenings at her house, which she called 'Coffee Squashes'. We did get Scripture lessons as part of the curriculum from priests and curates, one being Rev. Uphill from St.Mary's, who took lessons at St Peter's.

What the DGS did engender was a pride in our school which I think we all shared. Fundamental to this was the strict rule about school uniform. Woe betide any girl whom Miss Fudge spotted walking home without a hat on! I did not carve out any spectacular career from my first class education because I married at the age of nineteen but I still correspond with three of my class mates and we meet up whenever I come to Devizes

Freda Vince (née Rossiter 1933-1938)

Continental visits

I FIRST WENT into the preparatory department at Braeside for one term to ease me into the big school. To go to the main school everyone had to pass the 11-plus, but there must have been means testing because a small number had to pay between £1 and £4 a term, which was taken to school, so it was public knowledge.

Miss Paradise, who taught music and geography, was very unpopular. Her music lessons consisted of class singing with her at the piano, and she would often pounce on someone to sing a solo. I have no voice so I suffered agonies. In the second year we had to choose between Latin and Geography; the choice for me was obvious and that is why my geographical knowledge is sadly lacking.

A school trip was arranged each year for a small group of those lucky enough to be able to go. I went to Bruges for a week, staying in a hotel, not a school or hostel as in later years. The cost even then seemed cheap – £7 for the trip and a maximum of 10 shillings allowed for pocket money. In my fourth year we went to Paris for three days, ascending the Eiffel Tower and visiting Versailles, and then on to Switzerland for a week, at a cost of £40. We stayed in Wilderswil near Interlaken and it was magical, making a life long impression at that age.

In 1938 some of us sixth formers went to the Corn Exchange in the summer holidays to assemble gas masks. In 1939 we were in the school hall helping with evacuation arrangements when we heard Mr Chamberlain's announcement of war on the radio. During my last year 1939-1940 we sometimes had air raid practices when we went into Big Lane which had steep sides. By the second year sixth there were only three of us taking Higher School Certificate, two of whom were boys, Tommy Dewsnap and Paul Opperman, who was later killed in the war.

The trip to Bruges 1935, on the ferry. Back: Tommy Dewsnap, ?; Middle: Stanley George, Joe Worth, Miss White, Ethel Stagg; Front: Mr Marshall

Even in the thirties there was talk of a new school to be built on the Southbroom fields and we used to wonder whether it would be in our time. I was pleased when my daughter went to my old school, still in the same place, but half way through her time the Grammar School ended and they all moved to the new Comprehensive School. I enjoyed my time at the school; we were well disciplined but we had lots of fun.

Margaret Worth (née Rendell 1933-1940)

Frogs and hair grips

I started at DSS in 1935. My form master and French master was Mr Beasly. Despite there being no French connection in the family, I always came top in French. Later we had 'Froggy' Lund. On one occasion there were a

DEVIZES GRAMMAR SCHOOL 1906 – 1969 39

Form group 1936-7. Back row (left to right): Brenda Mead, Marjorie Welch, Margaret Dyson, Pat Alcock, Mary Child; Middle row: Dewsnap?, Cannon, King, Goodman, Porch?, Miles; Front row: Ruth Hibberd, Kathleen Pickering, Miss White, Marion Offer

Form VA 1937-8. Back row (left to right): ? Davis, Dolores Alcock, Ada Bishop, Mary Fuller; Middle row: Butler, Desmond Perry, Dan Hibberd, Philpott, Douglas Craddock, ?; Front row: Marion Rogers, ?, Mr Lund, Peggy Newman, Margaret Rendell

lot of frogs outside. Then when Mr Lund entered, lockers were opened and pandemonium broke loose , with frogs all over the place! He went berserk until all the frogs were caught and put outside. As he walked round the class, one girl called Gabrielle Groves clipped her hair grip to the bottom of his jacket and then we all passed our grips to her until there were about twenty all along his jacket hem. At break time we watched him come out of the staff room, but they were all gone. We were never found out!

I loved every minute of school. I had a five mile journey on the bus, then a mile cycle ride to get home to Little Cheverell. When my satchel was loaded with books, it sometimes slipped over my shoulder and caught the handlebars and pulled me back down the hill again. Once when I was cycling to the bus stop, I noticed a beautiful tawny owl in the middle of the road. It had no noticeable injuries and must have flown into the wires. I picked it up and took it on the bus to school. Miss Robinson, our Biology teacher, had it stuffed and put in a glass case in the lab.

Betty Cawley (née Green 1935-1940)

AT THE AGE OF 81, I still call myself one of the 'old girls'. My two brothers were at the school in the early twenties and forties and my three daughters, Pam, Pat and Jane attended the school from 1963 to 1969. It was a pity that the Grammar School closed because so many generations of Devizes families went there. Perhaps if it still existed my nine grandchildren would have attended.

Joan Flint (née Davis 1935 – 1940)

The Wartime Generation

Nettles and lemon bread pudding

I STARTED at the main school in 1936 in the partition room, so when Miss White was taking a folk dancing lesson, we in Room 4 had lessons to music. On special occasions when more room was required the partitions were drawn back and the iron-framed desks with lift up lids, fixed seats and inkwells had to be pushed aside. A few children had fountain pens and pen and ink were the order of the day. One teacher had a way of relieving his frustration by giving a great bellow. Observing a large blot on a boy's French exercise book, he demanded, 'What is the meaning of this?' 'That's where you shouted, Sir', came the meek reply.

Until hot lunches started we ate sandwiches either in the hut behind the main building or in a little room in Braeside, a teacher presiding in each place. Once when Mr Jones was supervising, things got very noisy and he stood up and gave us a brief lecture on good manners, ending with the words, 'And when you eat with me I expect you to behave as I do'. Then as he sat down he knocked his plate flying to the floor! Being Mr Jones he laughed as heartily as the rest of us. The start of school lunches was quite a sensation. Mrs Maslen and her staff cooked in the little kitchen in Braeside and the meals were served in the Panel Room. On the first day Mr Roberts and Mr Lund hovered, showing great interest. One enquired of the other, 'Is there a pudding for them?' 'Oh yes' was the reply, 'lemon bread pudding'- not a great start but there was a war on.

On Fridays during the lunch break we had violin lessons. These were brief because Miss Dalrymple, the peripatetic teacher, was invariably late. On Mondays after school the Choral Society rehearsed under the leadership of Mr Leacy. I remember during a performance of Mozart's Toy Symphony one of the players dashing out between movements to top up the water in his bird warbler. During the Spanish Civil War a group of Basque refugees, eight children in colourful costumes, gave a concert in the Town Hall, and the Choral Society was invited to take part – such a contrast, not only in the music but also in appearance, with us in our navy gym slips and white blouses and the boys in navy blazers. One of the highlights of the year was the carol concert organised by Mr Howells and Mr Leacy, with a very good supper and community carol singing. On one occasion the invitation had a footnote –'Please bring A and M'. One hopeful asked, 'Does that mean Auntie and Mother?'

Pat Kennedy (1936-1941)

'Banking' and stumbling blocks

THE SCHOLARSHIP EXAM (later called the 11+) was anticipated with some dread by those expected to pass and indifference by those who were not. Luckily I was one of the former and duly passed to go up to 'the Sec'. The year was a good one for Bromham, as with me were Nina Fennel, Dennis Hard, Ivor Minty and Brian Turvey. We started at the time of the Munich crisis, all cycling to school, quite a convoy of us; there were about sixteen in total from Bromham. Those of us living in the centre of the village set off about ten past eight, picking up others from The Pound, Hawkstreet and St. Edith's Marsh as we progressed towards school. If we played around on the way we often heard the school bell as we struggled up Dunkirk Hill; there was then a frantic rush to get to our form room for registration and then to the school hall for morning assembly. We stood throughout assembly, boys and girls segregated in disciplined rows and waited for the staff to appear, followed by the Headmaster. Despite playing the piano for the hymns, Miss Paradise – her favourite was 'He who would valiant be'– seemed to be able to detect any misbehaviour behind her back. We thought she must have 'eyes in the back of her head'.

Many of us were overwhelmed with the facilities of the school – woodwork and metal work room and other subject rooms. Flush toilets we from Bromham and other villages had not experienced before; sanitation and mains water did not come to Bromham until 1963! What thrilled us most were the playing fields, even though they were situated at the other end of the town at Southbroom Park. By the time we got there it was almost time to return home, but we played semi-organised soccer with real goalposts.

The first year form rooms were in the huts – wooden buildings at the end of the school yard, 1A near the rest of the school , 1B near the canal. It always seemed unkind to me that four of the Bromham contingent were in 1B while poor Turvey was consigned to 1A. The form mistress of 1B was an attractive young lady from Yorkshire, Miss Robinson, while 1A was in the care of Miss White, who later married a former pupil Bob Paget, who came from Bromham.

Form VI 1939-40. Back row (left to right) Margaret Rendell, Ada Bishop, Paul Opperman, Tommy Dewsnap, Butler, Kathleen Pickering; Front row: Margaret Pearce, Mary Munday, Primrose Archard, Marion Rogers, Dolores Alcock, ?

By the time we returned to school after the summer holidays of 1939, war had been declared and this was to have a great effect on school life. Sharing the school with the Ursuline convent, we attended on Monday, Wednesday and Friday; they went on Tuesday, Thursday and Saturday. We had to carry our cumbersome gas masks at all times, which was difficult when riding a bike, together with school satchel and games bag. Clothes rationing made compliance with strict school uniform difficult, so some relaxation had to be made. There were frequent changes of staff as many male teachers were called up.

Through the efforts of Miss Paradise, the school adopted a ship and we contributed what we could from our rations, sweets, chocolate, cakes, even Brylcreem. These were parcelled up and we got letters of thanks from the captain and crew. We also became involved in knitting 'Six inch Squares for Soldiers' from odd balls of wool. These were then sewn together to make a warm blanket. I was not very good at knitting so my mother used to knit up no end of squares from wool left over from knitting jumpers.

'Banking' was an induction for first formers. It involved two older, usually second form boys, grabbing a first former , one each side , and then propelling him down the bank, the grassed area leading from the yard to the playing area. The victims would generally tumble in the process. On one occasion this was to have a serious consequence for me. Some of the older boys came to the rescue of the victim and during the resulting affray I was somehow kicked in the head and suffered concussion. During the next class, Miss Pennel became aware that I was not 'with it'; a doctor was called and I spent the rest of the week in bed. At the subsequent enquiry my friend Turvey was blamed for the whole incident and was duly caned.

In 1941 at the beginning of the fourth year I had a long illness and missed ten months of school, so when I returned I stayed in Form IV, thus meeting a new set of form mates. I was very much involved in soccer with both school and youth clubs, but I suffered an injury and ended up in hospital again, returning to school after the summer break with a steel brace down my spine. Mr Halliwell, who had been most concerned, arranged for me to sit my School Certificate at Christmas, after intensive revision at Bath Technical College, so I passed well, with exemption from London Matric. I have many times regretted that I did not stay on to take Higher School Certificate, but I now look back on the Secondary School with tremendous regard. How difficult it must have been in the war years for teachers to keep up the standard of education for which the school had long been famed! I shall always be grateful to them and was sorry, distressed almost, when the decision was taken to reorganise secondary education, particularly as my daughter Becky had gained a place and completed one year and was then thrust into the *maelstrom* of the comprehensive system.

Peter Amor (1938-1945)

'Dig for victory'

MY MEMORIES are of a school much disrupted by war. Mr Roberts and Mr Leacy were called up into the RAF, Mr Howells into the army. Other teachers came and went all too frequently. Geoffrey Bond recalled that his school report book contained no fewer than 52 teachers' signatures.

We were the first intake to occupy the huts built on the playground of the Bath Road building as an overflow. With the arrival of the Ursuline Convent with their black-habited nuns, even the school hall was used to accommodate classes. Some lessons were inevitably curtailed and we happily spent Thursday afternoons at the Palace cinema. Vivid memories remain of Mr Roberts' romance with the curvaceous Art mistress, Miss Toombs, of the Senior Mistress and History teacher Miss Buchan-Sydeserrf, who lived with her mother on the top floor of Braeside, and of the incomparable wartime deputy head, Albert Fenton Lund, for many years churchwarden at nearby St. Peter's church.

In the war years Devizes was much dominated by the military presence. There were gliders overhead and tanks and tractor-drawn guns passing through the streets. The town was full of soldiers, some coming direct from the Normandy beaches, as well as German and Italian prisoners of war. Some boys (and not a few girls!) became friendly with the American troops. One or two of us acquired some multi-coloured ties from them. Once we took a chance and wore them to school, but were severely reprimanded and sent packing, to return wearing the correct school tie.

Roy Gilbert, Brian Neal and myself had the exciting experience of flying over Devizes in an American army flying jeep. We had cycled to Roundway Hill one evening and got chatting to the pilot of the two-seater aircraft which formed part of a convoy bivouacked there. 'You guys like a flight?' he enquired. How could we resist? So, one at a time and unstrapped, we were whisked across the town. It was a flight to remember!

At one stage we reluctantly assisted Bill Bridewell, the caretaker, to 'dig for victory', on the field behind Braeside, cultivating vegetables for the school kitchen. Some of us went on summer harvest camps at Higher Bridmore Farm, Tollard Royal.

Yes, they were eventful years, but there is no doubt that our scholastic aspirations suffered greatly

Terry Gaylard (1939-1944)

Flax pulling, cider and the harvest camp

I STARTED at Devizes Secondary School in September 1940, a month after my eleventh birthday. The catchment area of the school was very wide; pupils were bussed in from Tilshead, All Cannings, Keevil, Seend amd Bromham, some of these villages being up to twelve miles away. Many of us cycled, preferring this to the restrictions of the buses, which tended to be normal scheduled services and not special school buses. If you lived more than three miles away, you had a free bus pass or a cheque of a few pounds a term towards cycle maintenance. I daily rode four and a half miles carrying my satchel and my PE or sports kit – plimsolls (daps) or football boots, white shorts and vest. No towel was included as there were no showers. If you did get dirty you sluiced off, using your handkerchief and water from the wash basins. In the early days of the war we also had to carry our gas mask, contained in a six-inch square box.

Most secondary school stories feature a tuck shop. Across the road from the main gates, Mrs Benger ran a sweet shop, which we used when we had money. I cannot remember restrictions in using it, despite the fact that we had to cross a busy road.

When I was in Form IIA, our form tutor was the formidable Miss Paradise, a middle aged spinster with a lugubrious voice. She was a strict disciplinarian and by the standards of the day a good Geography teacher. She was constantly addressing us in a deep voice – 'Now class—'. She drummed geographical facts into us by using blank maps—'Fill in as many countries in Europe as you can remember'—'Name all the rivers in Northern England'.

This particular cold winter when we could not go outside, the PE staff hit on the idea of mixed country dancing. This was anathema to me, and to do this hand in hand with girls was beyond the pale! So I and some others sat out for a number of sessions. I do remember that there was some communication home and I was teased by my father that the days were not far off when I should enjoy dancing with girls.

In the second year we had the first years at our mercy, subjecting them to projection down the bank at speed, with a drop of some five feet. Unfortunately on a particularly wet day, one or two of them muddied their uniforms, and complaints were made to the Acting Headmaster, 'Froggy' Lund. About six of us were hauled to his office to receive three strokes of the cane across the backside. No time for exercise books in the pants- it all happened so suddenly. I remember saying something about 'traditional initiation ceremony'; 'Frog's' reply was,' I won't have bullying, see son!' So for the first and last time I received corporal punishment and took the weals home to show the battle scars to my parents. My father and mother took it in good part, though I thought it a little unfair that many had been involved and so few punished.

In the second year the Arts stream began Latin while the Science stream took extra Science. I chose Latin; I am sure I would have floundered in the science section, as I was always happier with words than figures and formulae. I did not embark on Latin with a great deal of enthusiasm, and it was not until later that I realised how important Latin was to be for me in the future. Gaining top marks in the summer examinations, I received as my prize 'The Aldin Book of Outdoor Games', dealing with rugby, tennis, golf and cricket and embossed with the school badge in gold. At that time Prize Day was an internal event, a glorified school assembly, but under the new Headmaster it became a public and civic occasion held in the Town Hall.

While in the third year, during school time, groups of us did our bit for the war effort, flax pulling. The whole class was bussed to some fields on the road to Swindon for a day's flax pulling. Flax had to be pulled, not cut, as the most important threads were to be found at the base of the stalk and into the roots. Flax fibres were needed for parachutes and just outside Devizes was a factory to process the results of our pulling. For us youngsters it was back breaking work, but probably the worst part was the first day when, gloveless, we realised that pulling flax could seriously damage your hands. The first thing we did after getting home that day was to find a pair of gloves. It was still fun though – no lessons, the days spent in the open air with a picnic lunch taken under a hedge, and of course some messing about with clods of earth thrown, mainly at the girls! We must have worked for about a fortnight until the fields were cleared.

A teacher who joined when we were at the third year stage was Harry Bolwell, a local printer who had not been called up because of his job. He joined the staff as an unqualified PE teacher; he was an excellent gymnast and developed that side for those interested, but he did lack discipline. Once we were sitting on small mats for floor work when one wag at the back shouted, 'Right lads, we'll be off to Baghdad this morning!' The whole class collapsed. Harry used to send us off on cross-country runs, following on his bike. Many's the time a group of us would hide under the canal bridge until he had passed and then saunter back to the school in record time. I disliked distance running and felt that 220 yards

Form V with Mr Lewis 1940. Back row (left to right): Edith Minty, Betty Perrett, Christine Brockis, Cynthia Draper, Margaret Butler, Phyllis Blake; Middle row: L Crouch, Ralph Holt, L Wadge, P Bryant, R Feltham, J Wheatley, A Newport, L Hutton, H Wood; Front row: H Breach, Jean Robbins, Gabrielle Groves, Viola Hale, Mr Lewis, June Hibberd, Joan Davis, Betty Green

was long enough. But Harry did a great job at a time when there were few younger men to teach PE and Games.

In the fourth year we moved to Braeside. Our form room was on the first floor at the back. There was a specialist Art room and a Geography room but the other rooms were not specially equipped, apart from the Library. Braeside had its own ghost – 'The Grey Lady', and at least one of my contemporaries swore he saw her. Others talked about the school bell in the hall ringing when there was no one about. We had some new teachers , such as 'Duke' Scruton whose nickname came from his nasal likeness to the Duke of Wellington. I remember we had medicals in the fourth year; the doctor examining me poked his finger in my stomach, saying, 'Get rid of that'. Yet I was not unfit as I played all major sports.

Our schooldays were taking place against the backcloth of the war. Salisbury Plain was a huge training ground for allied forces, and the roads were filled with convoys of vehicles. We were regularly overflown by the Luftwaffe and I can still remember seeing the horizon alight at night as Bath and Bristol burned and hearing the unmistakable throb of German planes overhead. Like many small boys we were interested in collecting war souvenirs, shrapnel and cap badges. During the war, standing in school uniform near Wadworth's brewery, we saw hundreds of German POWs in tattered and filthy uniforms marching from Devizes station to the camp on the London Road.

At the end of the fourth year I had my first experience of a School Harvest Camp. With so many men in the forces there was a need to supplement the agricultural labour force, so during the summer holidays we stayed at Higher Bridmore Farm near Tollard Royal. There must have been about sixty of us, boys and girls. We were housed in stable dormitories and fed in cow sheds. We slept on palliasses under rough blankets in the stable lofts. Despite the primitive conditions, we loved it and we had so many laughs. In the evening we had sing songs and games. Derek Fisher, Don Sutton and I borrowed some clothes and

At wartime harvest camp

cosmetics from the girls and dressed up in 'drag'. We danced in the middle of the yard and were immediately named 'The Belles of Bridmore'.

At the end of the summer holidays 1944 it was back to school for our School Certificate year. What a time to be taking such an important exam! There were no study aids or counselling then; we just got on with it. This was also the year in which I started smoking.. Travelling on the bus to an away match against Marlborough Grammar School, accompanied by Mr Jones, we went upstairs where he could not join us because of his wooden leg, and started smoking. But seeing us in the conductor's mirror, he shouted, 'Gane, put that chimney out!' Later that year I gave up, preferring sports fitness to pseudo-sophistication, as sport was playing an increasingly important part in my life. I was now goalkeeper in the !st XI and enjoyed perfecting the double punch approach to the high ball centred across the goal mouth.

We all looked forward to the summer harvest camp, the last time at Higher Bridmore Farm. The most memorable part of that camp was VJ Day. We were in a remote part of Wiltshire so a group of us decided to ride off and find a pub. We found a small inn, crowded with villagers, drinking rough cider. We joined in with the rest of them singing songs and downing pints. (I was fifteen). When it was time to go, the cold air hit us and the rough cider really took effect. Like Jacques Tatti as the drunken postman trying to cycle home, we fell off into ditches, re-mounted, then fell off again. When we got back the staff were waiting for us! We were helped up the ladder and put to bed with a drink and some sandwiches, but we were torn off a strip the next day, which did not do our throbbing heads much good, and our parents were informed, though no disciplinary measures were taken. Perhaps VJ Day was a good excuse for our excesses.

The end of the summer holidays brought the results of our School Certificate examinations. In those days you needed five credits to gain matriculation exemption and so be eligible to go to university. Unfortunately, our Latin teacher tried too hard to interest us and we spent most of our time drawing RAF squadron badges and then translating the Latin motto, not the best preparation for Caesar's *Gallic Wars*! I gained the required credits but failed Latin, which I needed to read arts at university, so I had to re-sit the exam.

In September 1945 I entered the Sixth Form of what now became known as 'The Grammar School', after the tripartite reorganisation of secondary education by the Education Act of 1944. We now had a new Headmaster, 'Jim' Halliwell, a smart dresser, who wore a navy blue striped suit with a different tie each day; clothes were rationed, so it was probably his demob suit. Our Head Boy, Geoff Bond, once said to him after assembly, 'Sir, we feel you have let us down today!' 'Why is that?' said Jim. 'Well, you've worn the same tie two days running'.

My last year at school was very enjoyable; I was now a Prefect and thinking of my future plans. Because I enjoyed a good argument, I decided to apply to do a BA in English Literature and Philosophy. The Head had asked me to coach some of the juniors in athletics, which I very much enjoyed and it was this which inclined me towards a teaching career, after I had done my national service.

Seven years at Devizes Grammar School had given this village boy a first class education, opportunities in sport and games, responsibility to shape character, life-long friends, a wider vision of the world and a taste of a vocation to come. I look back on those grammar school days with nostalgia and much affection.

Victor Gane (1940-1947)

Bread and butter before cake

WHEN MR LUND CAME to Bromham School to interview me for the final part of the 11+ exam. we sat out in the playground and he said, 'So Alice Powney is your mother?' I nodded, 'And Maureen Humphries is your sister?' I nodded again and that was that. He gave me a section of 'Drake's Drum' to read and asked me the meaning of the word 'lethargy', which I didn't know, and I was in!

Alice Powney was indeed my mother and she had started at the Secondary School in 1914. She became Head Girl and was among the first names on the honours boards, as was her sister Edith, another Head Girl. When the war started in 1939, Alice took her daughters away from Birmingham back to the family farm in Bromham. I started at the Secondary School in 1942, cycling to school as did many others from the village, unless they went by bus to school in Calne. There

On the lawn at Braeside July 1945. Back row (left to right): Pauline Doel, Joy Davis, Cynthia Sheppard, Jean Locke, Sybil Davis; Front row: Iris Flower, Margery West, Marion Jones, Marian Haines

were still two teachers at the school who had taught my mother, Mr Lund and Miss Paradise, who frightened me, and most others, to death. Once I was among the chosen few asked to tea with her. Her father served us, wearing a little apron, and we had to eat all the bread and butter before being allowed any cake. As this was war-time and things were tightly rationed, I suppose it was to be expected.

I remember the walk between school and Braeside and the strict path we had to take when crossing the road – below Shane's Castle towards school, above it going to Braeside. I remember the thrill of crossing where I liked as a prefect. Another 'perk' was being allowed to use the lodge; having our own private world made us feel very important.

I loved English and was awarded the senior school prize one year. I loved History, too, and remember how Miss Buchan-Sydeserff paced unremittingly up and down the classroom as she dictated endless notes. Mrs Jervis made it much more interesting but was nevertheless a strict taskmaster. Miss Tiddy taught me Domestic Science for which I am eternally grateful, even if I failed my School Certificate for allowing my cauliflower to boil dry!

I remember when Mr Halliwell came to pull the school together. I was immensely impressed by his first assembly. 'There are some among us who are stumbling blocks to progress', he said, 'and I am going to get rid of the stumbling blocks'. Sure enough some of the school clowns were no longer to be seen stringing bicycles in trees, tying blind cords to blackboards or throwing satchels over the wall.

Pupils from our year have had three very successful reunions, so we have really enjoyed being classmates again. We seem to have a fellowship which can only be attributed to the good old DGS.

Sybil Amor (née Humphries 1942-1949)

A love of the theatre

HAVING ENTERED the teaching profession in 1972 after a mature student course, I quickly realised how dedicated the teachers at DSS had been in the war, as many of them had to combine teaching with such duties as Air Raid Warden, while others started the Devizes branch of the Air Training Corps. They still managed, however, to lead many out of school activities such as music, drama, debating, verse speaking, the Christian Union and even bee-keeping.

Drama was my *forté* and in 1944 Richard Scruton decided to revive the dramatic society, which had begun in 1909 with a production of 'A Midsummer Night's Dream', when the tickets were priced at one shilling or sixpence. The

Form V with Mr Scruton 1945

Second World War, however, interrupted dramatic activities. The first post-war production was two one act plays, followed by a three act play, 'Distinguished Gathering'. As a junior in the audience, I thought it was very exciting and sophisticated. The following year I joined the dramatic society and was in three plays, 'Dangerous Company' and two costume plays 'Berkeley Square' and 'I have five daughters'. It was great fun, despite Mr Scruton being a strict disciplinarian, but we still managed to sneak out to the prefects' lodge to make tea when we were not 'on stage'. We all walked home together in the dark after a late rehearsal.

What was so good about the society was that it not only needed actors but stage crew, seamstresses, make-up artists and front of house personnel, which generated a great team spirit. I just remember a very happy time which fostered a lifelong interest in the theatre.

Lorna Bishop (née Bush 1942-1948)

The Prefects' Court

THERE HAS BEEN a general tightening up of the prefect system, with Miss Sydeserff as the prime mover – I wrote a first draft of a list of rules for the school—now we feel we have got some power behind us, we can get on and do something. I'm not sure all the staff approve of the new system.

Paul and Johnstone and I went up to town on Thursday and Paul and I on Friday, to see if we could catch any people without hats, and got quite a list. The penalty was to write thirty lines of a Shakespeare play and on Friday they had to do an essay of two pages on various subjects.

On Tuesday Miss Sydeserff gave us some DSS badges to put on our caps and on Wednesday in the detention assembly we were each presented with a small metal badge to put on our coats. It has the borough arms, with 'Devizes Secondary School' round the edge, colours blue and gold.

On Wednesday we had our first prefects' court. There were about a dozen offenders, most of them called for not wearing their hats or for refusing to do impositions for not wearing their hats. Moore, Gaylard and Bodman were released as we couldn't prove anything against them. The others had punishments such as polishing the benches in the Physics lab. or helping the cooks. Breach, who had written a sonnet libellous against the prefects, had to write another on 'Soap'. On the whole the prefects' court has been successful if unpopular.

1936 Extract from the diary of the late Tom Blake, 1943 (1936-1943)

'Froglin' and a big round zero

THE SCHOOL was really quite small and crowded, particularly on wet days when the morning break had to be spent indoors. One boy called Shotliff was always being chased by a group of lads around the boys' lavatories amid much banging of cubicle doors. On the whole I preferred to sit out these winter break times and eat some toast left over from breakfast.

Mr Johnson taught Maths. He was a neat, dapper man who spoke quietly. When he read out the Christmas term exam results, I was awarded 4% for Algebra and, as Mr Johnson said, 'A big round zero for Geometry.' A total of seven marks out of 300 must stand as a record to this day! Mrs Kennedy was kind in contriving to give me 50% for the Latin exam. Peter Flower said, 'Well done Froglin, I've got 50 as well'. My nickname 'Froglin' started when I was introduced to the railway station foreman by Chris Merrett, saying I had a double-barrelled name. The porter said, 'Like Froglin-Smith?' and somehow the name stuck. only to be enhanced by 'Foghorn' when my voice broke.

The Headmaster, Mr Halliwell, taught us General Science in the small lab. which had raised seating so that we could all see the experiments. We had this lesson after lunch, coming in all hot after playing outside. The Head always described the water used in the lesson as 'cool water', which caused a great thirst in the class. One day a series of acid batteries appeared on the bench and Mr Halliwell asked a boy called Cooper to connect them up. Two minutes later the Head returned to see each battery wired up black to red. 'Wretched boy,' he said, 'you've shorted the lot'.

During war time many teachers had to take subjects that were not their speciality. Mr Gobat taught us History, though his real subject was Art. One day when he was reading about the Saxons, a warrior was described as 'having blue eyes and blond hair'. 'He must have looked like Veronica Lake', said Mr Gobat. Only an artist could have said that with a complete disregard for the gravity of the subject. Mr Gobat was also in charge of our football games at Nursteed Road, which he seemed to enjoy, laughing quite a lot. He had a long face and little hair, which gave him the appearance of a rather sad clown, but his long scarf made him look like a student. Because of petrol rationing, he was unable to use his Morgan three-wheeler, so he was forced to cycle, pushing hard with his heels against the pedals which made it look like hard work.

I was out of my depth in most lessons but I did enjoy the school dinners, especially the puddings – jam tart, rice or bread puddings. The dinners were served by Sixth Formers, one of whom used to take delight in wheeling in puddings on a trolley at great speed and then bringing the whole thing to a sudden stop. I waited for him to tip the whole trolley up, but he never obliged.

Bill Crosbie-Hill (1944-1945)

Post War

Learning by osmosis

AT DGS I WAS HOPELESS at Maths, my main memory being Mr Lewis's ability to draw a perfect circle on the blackboard, freehand. Quadratic equations and logarithms were a form of torture and nearly as useless as Latin. I knew even less about Science, though from the fact that there were three different laboratories I remembered that Physics was about levers and things, Biology was about living things, while Chemistry was where I met Mr Jones, a bushy-eyebrowed Welshman who had been gassed in the Great War. I remembered little about Chemistry; there was something called H_2SO_4 which smelt and I was urged to learn that 'acid plus alkali equals salt plus water', though

DGS football team 1946-1947. Back row (left to right): Trapp, ?, Smith, Flower, Yates, ?, Mr Scruton; Front row: Davis, Hunt, Gale, Jones, Gane, ?, ?

I never let that impinge on my life. We watched Faraday's experiment being recreated, and I was delighted to learn that someone originally asked, 'What use is it?' (my kind of question) and was duly humbled by the reply from Faraday, 'Of what use is a new born baby?' Though he taught me little science, Mr Jones made me think – how did a soldier become a pacifist, as he had? When he died, many of us attended his funeral at the Methodist church and I can still remember the effect of singing the Welsh hymn 'Ar hyd y nos' with the refrain 'All will be well'. Our Head Girl, Pauline Newland, a Roman Catholic, attended her first Protestant service that day. Later we married, having both become pacifists, as we are today.

Another Welshman, Tommy Watkins, supervised our sport, all the while deploring the fact that it did not, then, include rugby. Saturday morning soccer matches were the highlight of the week for many of us, travelling to such unknown places as Swindon and Trowbridge, for during the war petrol rationing limited our movement. Trowbridge was where our soccer team encountered the late, great John Atyeo, later of Bristol City and England. I have often sat in the stand at Ashton Gate named after him. He too became a school master. Though Mr Leacy taught me little Physics, he did teach me the importance of bowling on a length, and thanks to DGS teachers I was able to enjoy both soccer and cricket competitively until I was fifty-five.

Upper and Lower Sixth boys Autumn 1947. Back row (left to right): P Hoddinot, ?, J Newland, A W Bennett; Front row: A Jones, C Thompson, D G Knapman, D J Davis, ?

Miss Janaway taught me to love History sufficiently to study it at university, Miss Guy taught me to love the novel and poetry, Mr Scruton to love drama. A group of teachers combined to support the annual school play, where minor miracles were performed on that tiny stage. We even went 'on tour' to Burderop Park, a teachers' training college near Swindon. When in the Sixties, I was thrust unexpectedly into the headship of a 800-strong school in Sarawak, I had little formal training in education, so I fell back on my experience at DGS. Our report books were copied from Mr Halliwell's, we did an annual school play and even took it on tour to a teachers' training college, though to get there we had to travel, and sleep, on the deck of a small ship across the South China Sea. So DGS was successfully transferred to the Equator. In 2003, as part of my wife's 70th birthday present to me, I was fortunate to return to meet my former students, seven of whom presented me with books that they had written. But their happiest memories were of plays performed and of teachers' idiosyncrasies. I suggest that the best and most lasting education comes from interacting with charismatic teachers and learning by osmosis (one word I did remember from Biology – or was it Chemistry?)

Keith Wiltshire (1944-1951)

Form IIIA July 1948. Back row (left to right): M Hiscock, P Winchcombe, G Strong, T Iles, P Watts, J Reynolds, J Frost, J Foyle; Middle row: T Wakeham, G Huntley, M Neate, Ann Farr, M Goodship, Mary Baker; Front row: Ann Dunnett, Shirley Fox, Janet Snook, Margaret Dobson, Miss Lacy, Margaret Stone, Aline Bolwell, Jane Poulsom, Norma Webster

Soccer and rugby memories

I REMEMBER Tommy Watkins particularly because sport was my main interest at School. For two seasons I often played soccer for the school on a Saturday morning and rugby for Devizes in the afternoon. The school rugby team was established in the autumn of 1952 and I was proud to be captain of a XV which won more games than we lost in our first term of rugby. We played cricket and football matches against other Wiltshire grammar schools and we appreciated Tommy Watkins and other staff giving up their Saturday mornings to take us to matches.

Philip Winchcombe (1945-1952)

Cricket XI, winners of the Grammar Schools Cup 1950

Tennis Team 1952. Back row (left to right): Naomi Drewitt, Shelagh Newland, Heather Sheasby, Pauline Newland, Jean Harding, Miss Greenwood; Front row: Pauline Cox, Kathleen Dight, Mary Ellis, Gillian Huntley

Long and full days

I OFTEN had long days at school. I would leave home at 7.45 a.m., cycle from Honeystreet to Woodborough station, take the train to Devizes, then walk from the station to reach assembly by 9 a.m. Because of choir and orchestral practices, drama rehearsals and events such as the Wiltshire Music Festival. I often did not get home till 7.45 p.m.. Then there was homework to do after supper!

Gill Winchcombe (née Huntley 1945-1952)

Meandering memories

MY EIGHT YEARS at DGS leave me with graphic, photographic recall which continues to give me pleasure today. So many teachers and classmates shaped my life and I am grateful for an education of which it is difficult to be critical. Material resources were limited at the end of the war, but we were tolerably well fed in the school canteen, and it was only in P.E. that there was, for me, any pain. Tennis shoes were unavailable and we had to scramble to find a laceless shoe amongst the hundreds in the lockless lockers while we changed for Physical Training.

In the late forties and early fifties, I felt greatly privileged to study at DGS with fifty or so students from the Devizes area, though it is only now that I realise that Philip Winchcombe and I were the only children from St Peter's to attend in 1945. Our hard-working teachers were much appreciated. 'Froggy' Lund Gladstone-bagged his way into student hearts, despite his requirement that homework should be parentally signed, something which provided potential business for a would-be class forger. Mr Lewis, as storekeeper, silently replenished exercise books and his teaching gained me a credit in School Certificate. My mother remembers Mr Lewis's beautiful wife, who, accompanied by their faithful dog, walked every day from Nursteed Road to Braeside to tryst at 4 p.m. Mr Lewis's urgings to me to attempt a cure for my verbal diarrhoea had a profound and lasting effect on my whole life, though more intimidating for me was 'Leaper' Leacy who taught Physics and called pupils 'Topsy' or 'Boy'.

Gradually younger teachers appeared. Mary Jervis, who taught History and PE, was a war widow with two gorgeous daughters. She had smiles for everyone, especially the Head Boy, Bawn, whom she eventually married. I secretly adored Jane Lacey, but when she sat with Maurice Goodship to help him with his mapwork, I felt pangs of envy. But not for long! My febrile affections

The staff 1950

transferred to two ladies who joined the staff in 1951, Lorna Read (History) and Margaret Davies (French) Their kindness, encouragement and selfless tutoring inspired me to aim at university. They warmly motivated me and I am ever in their debt, as I am to Miss Janaway and Miss Guy.

In September 1950 Miss Janaway did not return from holiday. We were horrified to learn that she was dying of cancer. She had been a most kindly influence in our lives and had a lovely sense of humour, which unfortunately did not extend to oranges. She was allergic to the smell and some students took advantage of this. She always wore her hair in two buns. When I visited Miss Guy, then aged 85, in her home at Mudeford, she had a book of cuttings about the acting career of David Ponting in the States, which brought back marvellous memories of drama days on stage at Braeside. I learned so much from Mr Scruton's brilliant productions – *Lady Windermere's Fan*, *Dear Brutus* and *Pygmalion*, which were great lessons in discipline, stagecraft and organisation.

In my eight years at DGS, I experienced innumerable instances of kindness and love. To some Devizes may have seemed a backwater, but I thought that the administration of Devizes Grammar School under Frank Halliwell and Denys John nothing short of great.

Terry Iles (1945-1953).

VIth form 1950. Back row (left to right): Mary Swift, Sam Reeves, David Lawes, Philip Adams, David Davies, Vernon Moger, Keith Wiltshire, Peter Lawes, Kathleen Dight; Front row: Sonia Boothroyd, Ina Russell, Pat Young, Joan Osland, Ruth Stevens, Pauline Newland

Scruton and Ancient Pistol

IT WAS A GREY DAY in 1951 when 'Old Scruton' was taking a disinterested Form IVA for English Literature on the canteen stage. We were slowly reading through the set play for that year, *Henry V*. It was like walking through treacle and most of the class were bored stiff with the difficult text. We had reached the tavern scene, Act 2, Scene 1. Mavis Alkins was reading Mistress Quickly, Bill Dowse was Corporal Nym and I was playing Ancient Pistol. Nym and Pistol were supposed to be arguing and Pistol was becoming angry, when I heard myself reading the fateful lines, 'For Pistol's cock is up and flashing fire will follow'. At that moment I caught the wicked glint in Mavis's eye; it was all too much for me and I burst into uncontrollable laughter. Scruton went puce; he went scarlet! With trembling finger he ordered me off the stage and then outside.

I never did make my peace with Scruton; from then on we hated each other. Unfortunately he was my form master as well so I got terrible reports from him ever after. After some fifty years I still feel aggrieved that I had been so castigated for reacting to one of Shakespeare's jokes. With hindsight I think Scruton was probably more embarrassed than we were . But what else would you expect from a mixed class of fourteen year olds?

Roger Swift (1947-1952)

Part of a school group 1951

Sport, surveying and Snob's Horse

I RECALL spending much of my time playing rugger, soccer and cricket for the school teams, with the occasional hockey match of boys versus girls. It was great fun to travel to other schools in the county and to the RAF base at Yatesbury. We had rowdy sing-songs on the way home. In addition there was always great rivalry between the houses at sports day and the cross country event. Initially the changing facilities at Southbroom were spartan but during my time showers were installed.

Probably one of the most notable achievements during my time at DGS was the discovery of Snob's Horse on Roundway Down with Peter Greed and Roger Swift. In a dry period and with the light in a particular direction, it was possible to see much of the outline. We measured it all up, but could not excavate because of the resistance of the farmer. But in the 1990s a site was found on

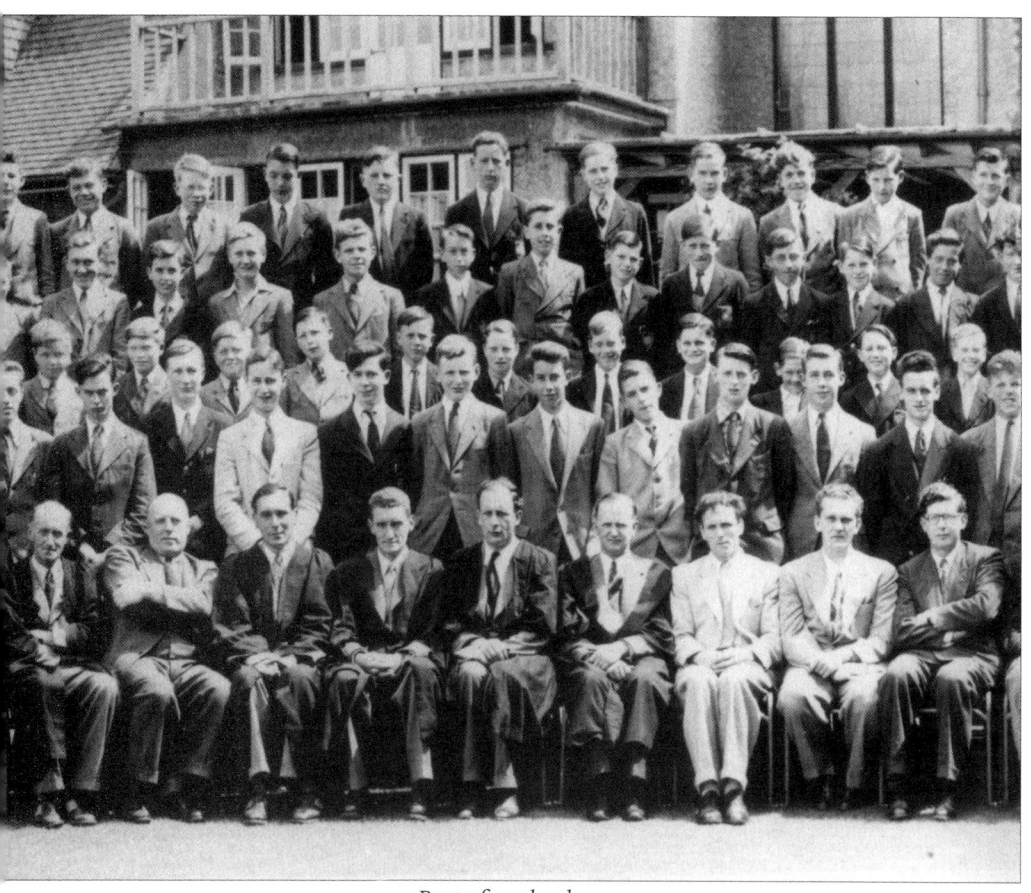

Part of a school group 1951

which to carve the horse as a commemoration of the millennium, although it was turned in the opposite direction.

By 1953 I was Head Boy and at the prize giving that year Shelagh Newland and I had to give responses to the address by the Bishop of Salisbury. Little did he know how much sweat and toil went into our compilations, but we left sufficient gaps to be filled in on the day to make it all appear spontaneous. Later that year I had to speak on behalf of the school at the first OSA reunion since the war. At the 1957 reunion as an old student myself, I referred to those who kept our grounds and buildings in good condition – Messrs Bridewell, Gingell, Osland and Rutter, who cheerfully moved furniture from one building to another across the busy road. We also had an excellent canteen staff who, despite the difficult post-war conditions, served up appetising meals at 5d. a head. For extras, we had the tuck shop run for many years by Mrs Benger and her daughter Heather, who made green pistachio ice cream and, in the strawberry season, ice cream incorporating chunks of fresh fruit. Many a secret was passed to the ladies about the school and its staff, but the students knew they would always find a sympathetic ear.

Form group c. 1951-1952. Includes Janet Alexander, Pauline Cox, Mary Ellis, Margaret Hampton, Susan Turner, Joan Watts, Tony Coleman, John Collett, Bill Dowse, David Ponting, Roger Swift, Will Worsdell

Kitchen staff, caretakers and gardeners 1950s

For several years I recorded the rainfall under the guidance of Mr Clook, who must have tabulated the results somewhere. For the last twenty-five years I have recorded the rainfall where I now live. I was really only good at two subjects – Maths and Geography, which influenced my choice of career. I think only myself and one other from DGS – Tom Welsh – entered the small profession of land surveying. While I was in the Sixth form, Mr Clook one day showed me a circular about a course at a Field Study Centre near Dorking. I went – and was hooked, and set up for the rest of my working life.

There must be a common thread running through many of my reminiscences and it is that many aspects of school life, some only a minute or two a day such as measuring the rain, help to nurture useful activities in later life. School life was not just about the three Rs, but a myriad of smaller, almost unnoticed activities learnt along the way that led to what one hopes has been a more useful life.

Jim Smith (1946-1954)

Exploding dustbins

SMARTLY DRESSED in grey shorts, blazer, tie and cap with my satchel and gym bag, I arrived at the boys' entrance to start my secondary school days. We were ushered into the large assembly hall. There on the wall were the honours boards, listing the students who had been successful in gaining state scholarships or county scholarships.

Someone started to play the piano and the staff filed in wearing their gowns, and once they had settled the Headmaster, Mr Halliwell, came to the rostrum. Daily assemblies consisted of a bible reading followed by a hymn and announcements. For the first and final assemblies of the term the same passage was read; I always return to those assemblies whenever I hear that reading – 'Though I speak with the tongues of men or of angels, but have not charity I am become as sounding brass or tinkling cymbal'.

Certain of my first lessons come to mind – the cross section of the buttercup and it being able to have corm or bulb, and 'Daddy' Burt's introductory woodwork lesson, illustrating his skill with wooden joints, which were as sturdy and strong as himself. I still have the garden basket, the three-legged stool and the bill/invoice hook which were mandatory in completing his very structured skills course. Then there was the time when the Chemistry teacher Mr Jones was not well and the lesson was taken by the Headmaster, a person we usually only saw at morning assembly on his rostrum. He taught us to determine whether or not the prism which had come from the turret of a World War II tank was solid or hollow.

Our first three years were based in the Bath Road building and emphasis was placed on academic work. Apart from the initiation ceremony of 'banking', time seemed to pass seamlessly. The 5th of November pranks usually culminated in the use of thunder flashes, obtained after the war. These were usually placed in an 'empty' dustbin, down near the boiler room, the lid was replaced , then 'boom'! Students in the upstairs window recorded the height to which the lid ascended. Of course such activity required the use of look outs to ensure the caretaker was out of sight (certainly not out of sound!).

Playground games consisted of 'kingy' and various wall games like 'Hi Jimmy Knacker', where one student would lean down with hands on the wall and successive boys would jump on the preceding student's back, then lean down behind, forming what looked like a caterpillar, head against the wall, with boys attempting to jump as far down the length of backs as possible.

Art teacher Mr Gobat's ink smudgings always fascinated me – how he could produce such shapes and wonderful landscapes from just small ink drawn lines, which he then smudged with his thumb, was a wonder to me. My efforts always seemed to look like smudged ink lines. He was kind enough to reproduce one in an autograph book for me. Mentioning thumbs will, I am sure, cause other students to recall a particular member of staff, who always seemed to be thumbing his lower lip as if strumming it downwards. 'Froggy' Lund, our French teacher, would always strum his lower lip before turning over the next page of text. He lived at the end of Salisbury Street off the Bath Road. Our routes to school corresponded and as I walked to school he would pass me on his black upright bicycle, fitted with one of the old clarion bells, with his attaché case either in the forward basket or on the rear carrier. Then there was Mr Scruton, the English teacher, who had the first joint of one forefinger missing and we always wondered whether it was the result of a war wound. We knew that Mr Clook had indeed survived an aircraft accident when flying in South Africa and had suffered a serious skull injury.

Physical Education took a regular place in the curriculum, with two single lessons in the main hall and an afternoon of games for us juniors on the field at the back of Braeside. Mr Watkins used to delight in taking us for cross country running which he liked but most of us didn't. He used to cycle with us, claiming that he had just been running with the previous group, but the bicycle always seemed to be in evidence. I recall one particular PE lesson using the box and jumping platform. He started placing benches between the take-off platform and the box. After four or five benches had been introduced we refused to attempt the jump. He accused us of being 'yellow' – we admitted we were – and that was the end of the lesson. When we were seniors, the games afternoon took place at Southbroom and students had to make their own way during the lunch break, and afterwards back to Braeside for those who travelled by bus. Some sixth form students had the benefit of using the squash courts in the Market Place.

The canteen was used as a base for the boys' cross country. I was far from a keen cross country runner and neither was Tony Duck. Still, everyone had to take part. One particular year Tony and myself, ensuring that everyone was in front of us, came to the final corner near the canteen. The race finished on the field at Braeside and I now readily admit that I nudged Tony into the prickly bush at the corner of the building, thus ensuring that he was last, which he always professed he would be. As was the custom, senior responsible girls were asked to volunteer to fill numerous small baths in the canteen with hot water in preparation for the boys to wash down. There was never any lack of volunteers as the girls knew that the two service hatches between the kitchen and the canteen were not well fitted!

In our fourth year we were based at Braeside. Just inside the entrance was the complete senior school time table, meticulously drawn by Mr Lewis and colour coded for subjects. Ours was the first year of the GCE and we were urged to do well in this exam. I passed five of my six subjects but failed Latin, which I needed to go to university, so the following term I had extra lessons with 'Ego' Howells on Saturday mornings. He also taught music and encouraged participation in the school choir. Like many others, I have fond memories of the Christmas carol concert in the canteen, the procession into Braeside, the carrying of the Boar's Head, complete with apple in the mouth, to the sumptuous spread before a roaring log fire in the inglenook fireplace where the room was decorated with a Christmas tree. The canteen was used also for the school plays. I assisted John Reynolds with sound and lighting and I was in charge of the dimmer controls. Ever since, I have associated *Eine Kleine Nachtmusik* with ice cream, for it was the music played in the intervals. I was involved with every production on stage or behind the scenes until I left in 1954.

Due to the small number of students involved in each year of the A level Science courses, upper and lower sixth students were taught together. It was a huge academic jump for us from GCE. We had two double theory lessons plus a three hour practical in the afternoon, which did not finish till five o'clock. We had to carry out an experiment, write it up and have it marked before we could leave. Mr Patterson, our Physics teacher, inspired in us a wonder of the scientific world. He also ran an electronics club after school, where I built my first mains powered radio receiver. John Reynolds made a new audio power amplifier for the stage audio system. Each year we looked forward to Mr Patterson inviting his sixth form physics students to his house for tea.

Mr John, our new Headmaster, took some of the sixth form to visit his previous school, the independent boarding school, Bedales. As we were walking though the grounds there, a group of students came up and addressed him as 'Denys'. Students having the effrontery to address our headmaster in this way was a huge culture shock for us!. Mr John was keen to encourage italic handwriting, and one of his students, Pam Lacey, won a prize in a competition, which he had great pleasure in presenting to her at morning assembly.

Mr Patterson, Mr Beasley and Mr Scruton 1951

Prefects were also presented with their badges at assembly. The new girl prefects constructed multi-braided tassels in the school colours to be attached to the centre tag of berets or caps. Use of the prefects' lodge was one of the privileges we enjoyed, a coal fired stove enabling us to cook toast or crumpets. The location was also convenient for supervising the student bus queues, another of the prefects' duties.

Nearby were the school gardens, with wonderful displays of flowers along the main drive, and at the rear of the building were the vegetable gardens which supplied vegetables for school dinners. The woods and the grounds made a very pleasant background to our school days.

Peter Greed (1946-1954)

A School Journey; some reminiscences after nearly sixty years

THE LONG AWAITED DAY arrived early in September 1947. I was to join my father, sister and a school friend Pam in travelling on the Wilts and Dorset public service bus from our village of Wilcot on a circuitous route to

Devizes. Pupils were picked up at various stops, those going to the Grammar School distinguished by their navy uniform and maroon striped ties, caps for the boys and berets for the girls. We were dropped off outside Braeside entrance and guided to the lower school entrance across the road.

Pam and I found seats next to each other in Form 1A, surprised to discover that in one class there were more pupils than there had been in our entire village school, and all about our age instead of ranging from 5 to 14. A strict timetable was new to us. There would be no more leisurely walks along the Kennet and Avon canal banks just because the sun shone! We had different teachers for different subjects and changes of room for certain lessons, whereas there had been only two classrooms in our old school. The first year forms were housed off the main hall, which served as a venue for whole school assemblies and could be transformed into a gym. The boys and girls were separated for woodwork, domestic science and P.E. and games, and this provided us with an opportunity to get to know the rest of our year. A coach took us to Southbroom playing fields, a vast, tree-edged green area for soccer, rugby, cricket, hockey, rounders and athletics. Hockey and athletics were to feature strongly in my life. I liked nothing better than to charge up and down the hockey pitch in all weathers. In the summer we walked to the open-air swimming pool, where low temperatures tested the enthusiasm of those who had not learnt to swim. But things improved as the summer progressed and it became a welcome outing, with Mrs Jervis urging the girls to achieve their first width.

School dinners in the canteen at Braeside inspired a new vocabulary for some items on the menu – for example 'ollies 'eads' for sultanas in semolina. The set hot meal was standard fare for its time, meat and two veg., stewed fruit and steamed puddings and custard. Some of the produce came from the school gardens, and those of us who had to set out at 7.30 a.m. were hungry enough to relish these delights.

My friend Pam moved away at the end of our first year and there was a re-organisation of class membership at the start of the second year. Those who had shown a talent for learning French went into 2A, where Latin was introduced. In future years this was to mean that the A form dropped Domestic Science and Art. I have never seemed to catch up in Domestic Science but have compensated for missing Art by taking up painting in retirement. The third year saw our move to Braeside where we revelled in our form room with its back row seats in the inglenook fireplace and the freedom to roam the lawns, borders and woodland in the lunch hour or just lounge about. Clubs, such as choir, orchestra, library, chess and Christian Union provided us with other interests. On Saturdays there were sports matches, either at home or away. The Dramatic Society met after school and after many rehearsals put on accomplished performances of plays such as *I Have Five Daughters* and *Dear Brutus* under the direction of Mr Scruton. The Society went from strength to strength with the arrival of Mr Haycock in our fifth year, with productions such as *Thunder Rock, Merrie England* and *The Mikado*. These last two of course demanded musical talent and principal singing roles were brilliantly undertaken by Miss Davies, Mr Howells and Mr Moore as well as gifted pupils and old students, all supported by male and female choruses and the school orchestra. Miss Read contributed greatly by helping with rehearsals, costume and make up, while Mr Beasley was ingenious in the scenery and stage managing department.

The fourth and fifth years meant knuckling down to O levels and increased homework. At the same time, a few members of our class began to invent ever increasingly annoying ways to test the patience of the staff. Miss Read, the young and glamorous, newly arrived History teacher in her first post, soon had the measure of them. We had to write pages of dictated notes to catch up on missed syllabus and then we all became caught up in the lively, interesting presentation style of someone who had a thorough knowledge and love of her subject.

Those pupils who went into the lower sixth joined others of the upper sixth in their A level studies with a choice of arts or science subjects. I became an Arts student and had to face the challenge of the move from teacher-led lessons to more individually focussed and researched study. We were fortunate to be encouraged by our friendly, time-generous teachers who brought knowledge, dedication and humour to their teaching and who laid a sound foundation for future academic endeavour and life-long interests.

When not on lunch-time duty as prefects, we went to clubs, meetings or get-togethers in the form room or in the prefects' lodge at the bottom of the drive. Much mirth and, I dare say, gossip thus evolved. Friendships were sealed and many have stood the test of time. Small reunions have taken place since 1996 and we look forward to the Grand Reunion of 2006. Will we recognise each other in our seventies? Our paths may have diverged but we hold a common affection for our old school. And yes, dear reader, I became a teacher too!

Shelagh Way (née Newland 1947-1954)

Life-long friendships

THE FIRST FEW DAYS must have been daunting for those of who joined from small rural schools, where passing the 11-plus was quite an event! We soon felt quite at home, mothered by Mrs Jervis, who would help us knot our ties after PE lessons to present us tidily back to the classroom. We were proud of our uniform in those days. Beside the excitement of learning new subjects such as French and Latin, I remember the popularity of the game of Fives and the mad rush to bag the courts at break time.

Nowadays if I am awake to hear the introductory music to Radio 4 at 6.30 a.m., the traditional tunes such as 'Men of Harlech' and 'Scotland the Brave' take me back to the old canteen at Braeside where we had our music lessons. These lessons were looked upon as light relief with no homework at the end. Poor Mr Howells! But he would have been rewarded by the success of the choirs and orchestra at the Devizes Eisteddfods at the Corn Exchange.

I have very happy memories of my time at DGS, where many of my lifelong friendships were formed, and this is why some of us look forward so much to our small annual reunions.

Mary Bradley (née Ellis 1947-1954)

Boys, topsies and moving tables

NOT EVERYONE understood when I talked about my French mistress. But of course I was referring to my *French* mistress, the ferocious Miss Davies. On her first class with us she came into the room like a whirlwind and scattered all before her. It was rough and raw and you tried to get out of the way. But over the next few months and through exercising the time-honoured techniques of all naughty school children, we measured her up and discovered she was really a pussy cat; inside the velvet glove was a velvet fist.

Part of this mutual re-evaluation resulted quite early on in Miss Davies inviting a dozen or so sixth formers to a Christmas party at the house she shared with her mother. During that particular term we had a French *assistante* from Algeria, who was also invited. The party night came and good food, non-alcoholic drink and good company made for a most convivial evening, so that when some time around eleven o'clock Mrs Davies said she thought it was now time for the table, many of us were in a somewhat giggly and dismissive mood.

'Be serious, mind!' said Davies senior as we gathered round a smallish, four-legged side table and rested our hands on it, touching fingers with neighbours.

'Are you there?' she said, and the rest of us fell about.

A couple of minutes of total hilarity. Then at last – 'Shush! All right then. Just be believers.'

Among our student number was present one who claimed a belief in spiritualism and so just he and the Davieses settled down round the table.

'If you are there, tap twice!'

Nothing, followed by a bit of a giggle.

'If you are there, tap twice!' And to our amazement the table began to rock. 'Could three pairs of hands do that?' the rational side of me asked. Possibly. Anyway there was no tapping and the rocking stopped.

'If you are there, tap twice!' Again the rocking and the table went up on two legs, fell back and hit the floor. Then it did it again. Two knocks; we were gob-smacked!

'Do you have a message for someone here? Knock twice for yes and once for no.' Rocking, the table went up on two legs and crashed twice.

Miss Davies looked around at the now silent watchers. 'Is there anyone who doesn't want to hear a message if it's for them?' Nervously we all said no, hoping it would be someone else.

'Two knocks for male, one for female!' Up went the table, just once.

'We are ready!'

To my astonishment the table went up on two legs and began banging the floor with the speed of a machine gun. Mrs Davies called off letters alphabetically on each bang and at 'L' the table stopped. She repeated 'L' and immediately off it went again. This time it stopped at 'E'.

'Well', I thought, 'the message is in French!' But no! Up went the table again for a third letter 'T', and it would do nothing more until Mrs Davies had said 'Let', when off it went again. And so it went on until the whole message had been spelt out: 'Let Claude go!'

I turned to the French *assistante* to find that tears were streaming down her face. The table did not seem to want to do anything after that, but someone suggested that it should be asked to stand on one leg. And it did! And not just that. It spun on that leg, making several revolutions, before dropping to the floor, careering across the room and colliding with the door frame of the French windows where it stopped dead!

During all that fast action, three pairs of hands were hardly in contact and during its movement across the floor nobody was near the table. I turned it over. There were no strings and I could not see how or why this event could have been staged. But I swear that, even making allowances for the passage of time and brain cell death, it happened exactly as written here.

Most of us were too scared to go home by ourselves that night and arrangements were made to ensure that people went in groups. One person who had cycled several miles to the party simply refused to return home that way and a disgruntled dad had to be levered out of bed to take him home in a car, bicycle tied to the roof rack.

There, one might have thought, the story ended, but there was a postscript. Early the following term, Miss Davies told us that just before leaving for England, the French *assistante* had been unofficially engaged. Initially she had received weekly if not daily correspondence from her fiancé, but as Christmas approached, fewer and fewer letters came, and soon none at all.

But the day after the party, a letter from her beau was delivered. It was very apologetic and asked that their marriage understanding might be ended, as he had fallen for someone else.

And of course, his name was Claude!

I walked down Braeside drive towards the road and just before turning into the prefects' lodge, where only deep academic thoughts were thought and solid work was worked, I noticed that the large front gate had been pulled across the driveway and a sign writer was carefully painting the school's name.

Some time later, having worked solidly and thought deeply, I left the lodge, intending to return to that other seat of learning, the library. At that moment the painter was standing back to admire his work and I joined him. DEVIZES GRAMMER SCHOOL it said.

Now for all my schooldays I had been unjustly branded as a know-it-all-big-head, an image I had tried hard to put right. In any case, being a bad speller myself, I was very diffident when I suggested to the painter that perhaps his sign was not spelt correctly.

His face fell. 'Oh no!' he said, 'Is there only one M?'

In the summer of 1955, being a leaving sixth former, I thought it would be a good idea to do something different for my last house party. I had met a really talented man who could sing and play just like George Formby and I thought this would be ideal for a cabaret act. He was very modest about his skill and told me that he really only played for his own amusement. But a promise of ten bob seemed to make it all right, though I explained to him that I would have to clear it with the Headmaster. Next day I approached Mr John, who was very enthusiastic. So my George Formby sing-alike was set to feature in the forthcoming party. It was all arranged.

And then, on the morning of the event a somewhat worried Mr John approached me and said he would like a word. We went to his office.

'Your cabaret singer', he said, ' what sort of George Formby songs will he sing? I mean, he's not going to do the ones with words about – er – I mean – he will keep to the other ones, won't he? — Is the window cleaner going to feature?'

Actually he didn't need to go into detail; I knew what he meant. It had not occurred to me that some parents might complain about Formby's gentle innuendo.

Today it seems difficult to believe that 'My shirt's so short that it won't fit my —(pause)—little brother' might have given offence in 1955, But it could be that lines about a Chinese laundry might be considered racially offensive now.

Of course we went to school to get educated (Africa is a hot country, *amo, amas, amat* etc.) but most of the real education which has stayed with me over the years was achieved extra-curricularly.

There was Friday evening dancing class where we moved to music and, with Mantovani's help, found out exactly where and how a girl's outs and ins snuggled into a boy's ins and outs. I had not realised how much social assurance this particular aspect of education gave me until I saw the product of single-sex schools, standing embarrassed and alone at university hops. I cannot say how much I appreciate being spared all that.

And then there were trips to the theatre. Initially I went because my girl friend was going and I might be taken to the gates of Paradise in the back seat of the coach on the way home. She might even let me put my arm around her shoulder. But then I found that I was actually enjoying the plays we saw.

From a wealth of theatre visits, I pick out a couple; a delicious and thoroughly unprofessional giggling fit by Alan Bates and John Neville in a Bristol Old Vic production of 'School for Scandal', and, perhaps most precious of all, a matinée performance of some boring old fart's play called 'Twelfth Night'. On that afternoon I took my seat and glanced at the programme Two or three names caught my eye; hadn't I heard of an actor called Laurence Olivier. who was playing Malvolio, and a woman called Vivien Leigh? Though I remember nothing of Leigh's performance, with the rest of the audience I was in hysterics at Olivier's. The fact that Shakespeare was actually funny had never occurred to me before. And moving, and meaningful. It was a seminal experience.

Many years later when I was playing a minor role in a BBC production where Sir John Gielgud was the lead, I plucked up courage and approached the great man. I told him what an important turning point his production of Twelfth Night had been in my life so many years before. He turned to me and with that voice – 'like a trumpet wrapped in silk' – he said , 'Ah, dear boy, wasn't Larry awful? I mean really awful. It's not meant to be that funny. I just couldn't control him'.

Not only was I introduced at school to a life-long friend called William Shakespeare, but also to a special someone who cropped up in General English, a horizon-broadening but fortunately unexamined subject you had to take if you were in the Science Sixth.

This special young man's name was Dylan Thomas. I even bought his books before he was dead and found the humanity of those smutty, lavatory wall stories ('wombs with a view', he called them) appealed directly, not just to the hormone-soaked teenager of yesterday but also to the same teenager inhabiting this seventy year old body.

A Chemistry teacher called Leacy
Found remembering our names not easy
 So to keep his employ
He called all the boys 'boy'
And the popsies were simply called 'Topsy'.

The only other thing that sticks in my mind about Mr Leacy was his car. This was already old and battered when Ford was still a boy. Whether teachers' salaries were insufficient to get cars properly repaired and maintained or whether in this case Mr Leacy did not care enough, this car was a write-off and should have been scrapped long before. In the dust on the back of the car was written 'Buy a new batery'.

Each school day, however, Leacy would set out to drive it from his house in Rowde, fight with it on the slow climb up Dunkirk Hill, and having reached Braeside, he would gratefully turn left and allow the wreck to coast down the slope to its daily parking place beside the stables at the back of the house. Of course this meant when it didn't start in the afternoon (which was par for the course), the first problem was getting it up the rise to the forecourt.

At this time I was in the habit of leaving my bike resting against the stable wall just beyond his car; consequently I was daily press-ganged into joining a dozen or so little scruffs , 'to put back the potential energy the car lost when it rolled down the hill this morning'. This may sound as though a great effort was needed, but it was not. Don't think of an enormous car or even a mini. Think more of a Victorian pram. A puny first year could probably have lifted it with one hand. The problem was that Leacy insisted on sitting in the driving seat while we pushed, and he weighed considerably more than the car.

On no-start days and having achieved the front of Braeside, the pushers were allowed a brief breather before being required to race it down the drive to get the engine going. If we were lucky it would burst into life with a cloud of blue smoke, and we would run into a shower of oily black smuts which were hard to remove. And then with a distant wave of his arm, Leacy was gone until tomorrow. I always think of this experience as part of a good balanced education. I learnt something about potential energy. I learnt that it was better to leave my bike in the sheds behind the main building down the road. And as somebody pointed out, I learnt that there are two T's in battery.

David Ponting (1947-1955)

Contrasting headmasters

MY FIRST DAY at the school was probably the most memorable and probably the least happy. I was a late entry; straight into 1HB, halfway through the third term; no interview but with a reputation for recalcitrance. My instructions were to go to the Headmaster's study at 9.00.a.m. Arriving in the busy lobby at Braeside, which I had not previously visited, I sought directions from the only obvious figure of authority, who turned out to be Mr Leacy, a tall, kindly man with a booming voice. He took me to assembly in the main hall where he introduced me to Mr Halliwell. I immediately received a severe lecture on the necessity of following instructions precisely. This was not a promising start!

Mr Halliwell was an austere figure who was respected but not much liked by his pupils. It was standard practice among the boys to seek an escape route if one was on a path which meant passing him, as almost invariably some criticism would be suffered. One or other of us must have matured over the years as by the time he left we had established a reasonably friendly relationship.

For what was essentially an academic institution, a lot of time was spent on practical subjects. We had gardening lessons and a double period of wood and metal work. The workshops were presided over by 'Daddy' Burt, a man of infinite skill and patience. However he decided that his skills were no match for my ineptitude and I became the only fourth former to have a double free period. This time was spent reading in the library under the eagle eye of Miss Guy.

Sport was also an important part of the curriculum, with two periods of PE and a double period of games. As we had no proper gym facilities in the hall, PE was mostly done out of doors, irrespective of temperature and usually stripped to the waist. Tommy Watkins did not tolerate any slacking! Training for the compulsory cross country in the Spring often took place in falling snow and in the summer we swam in the town's outdoor, unheated pool. I certainly remember going in when the temperature was 54F.

One of the great strengths of the school was the breadth of education it gave us. In years one to four we were given a list of classic English novels which we were expected to read in addition to those being studied as set texts and there would be questions in the end of year exams on these. Trips to the theatre were regular if not frequent. Sixth Form pupils were regularly invited to the Headmaster's table and you were expected to be able to contribute to the conversation on current topics. In 1953 a trip to Paris was organised, at a time when private travel was unusual and most people's cultural experience was limited to the radio and the local cinema. Many, if not most, of the pupils came from comparatively simple home backgrounds and acquiring cultural and social skills was as valuable as formal education.

School uniform was always worn; cap and blazer, both with the school badge, tie and grey trousers, grey or white shirts. Caps and ties could be discarded for a specified period in the summer term. Fifth formers were excused caps and the sixth form were allowed a certain latitude, such as double breasted blazers and cavalry twill trousers. Prefects wore a distinctive tie. I have seen a prefect's cap which had a silk tassel on top, which might indicate that older boys had worn caps in the past. Caps were always raised to any member of staff who might be met outside school. Any misbehaviour in the street whilst wearing school uniform was not tolerated.

Although Mr Halliwell was an austere presence, discipline was lightly applied. The cane was available but I can only remember it being used on one occasion. The usual punishment for minor classroom offences was to be sent to stand outside the door. The only time it happened to me was doubly embarrassing as it was outside the Maths. room which was at the top of the stairs *en route* to both the staff room and the Headmaster's study. In my experience discipline was not a real problem; there was mutual respect between staff and pupils and the school was a happy place. It was, of course, the custom for the class to stand and greet the teacher at the start of each lesson, which established order immediately.

The sixth form tutor was a Cornishman named Patterson, who taught Chemistry. He always claimed that he believed in fairies. He used to stand in front of his A level group and say that his ambition was to teach us to read before we left; it was generally held that he was quite mad. It was only in later years that I, and probably many others, realised that most of us read what we thought should be on the page rather than what was actually there. On one occasion he opened a fume chamber before it had properly cleared and breathed in some of the content. A few minutes later he said, 'Duck, give me one of those cigarettes which we all know you carry in the case in your inside pocket, or I shall be sick'. He then continued teaching the lesson while smoking a Turkish cigarette – unconventional then, but probably a hanging offence now.

Mr John, Halliwell's successor, was as liberal as Halliwell was conservative, coming as he did from an *avant-garde* co-ed. boarding school. One of the first changes he proposed was that pupils should address staff by their first names, instead of Mr or Miss. I do not know what the staff position was on this but the prefects were quite adamant that it was unacceptable. Certainly it did not happen in my time.

At this time a number of older staff left. Many of them had stayed on beyond retirement age to help out with staff shortages caused by the war and National Service. Their replacements were often straight from university and not much older than their sixth form pupils. One arrival which caused a *frisson* among the older boys was Lorna Read, who discovered amongst them a previously unnoticed interest in History and ballroom dancing.

One of the strengths of the school had always been drama and this was carried forward by the arrival of Bert Haycock, who not only extracted performances far beyond the talent and dedication of his casts but also introduced a more adventurous repertoire. With Ron Beasley as Stage Manager and Lorna in charge of costumes and make-up, minor miracles of magic were regularly achieved on the tiny canteen stage for many years. For the pupils the benefits were to give them greater confidence and the ability to add value to a group effort.

Although leave was given for a two week period while external exams were taken, it was then back to school until the normal end of term, even for those of us who were leaving. But that last July was different. In 1953 it had been decided to create an outdoor theatre in the far corner of Braeside grounds to commemorate the coronation of Queen Elizabeth II. The school gardeners, helped by the senior boys, achieved this project in about three months, all done with shovels and wheelbarrows and no mechanical aids! There followed a memorable *Merrie England*, succeeded the following year by *The Mikado*, a wonderful end to my time at the school.

Tony Duck (1949-1954)

A trip to the Festival of Britain

MY FIRST MEMORIES of the school are of cycling from my home in Brickley Lane on my Hercules cycle; it weighed a ton! On my first day I remember someone, I think Tony Bartlett, a year or so older than myself, saying,

'Have you seen a chap with a face like the back of a bus?' To my astonished 'No', he replied 'Well, when you do, that's Froggy Lund'.

Sometimes Billy King or Michael Lee and I went on fossil gathering expeditions in the lunch hour on the sandstone cliffs at the bottom of Braeside gardens. On one occasion we arrived back late for lessons and were made to stand, pockets bulging with finds, outside the classroom. I kept this collection for some years afterwards.

In 1951 the school organised a trip to the Festival of Britain in London, exactly one hundred years after the Great Exhibition of 1851. This was one of the first signs of the relaxation of post-war austerity, with the futuristic Skylon, the Dome of Discovery and the South Bank exhibition. It was a revelation for a thirteen-year old boy. I became briefly lost in the Dome of Discovery, but not long enough to provoke a panic.

Never to be forgotten was Benger's tuck shop, with the sweets in jars and the famous ice cream. Sweets were the last items to come off rationing in 1954 and we all descended on Benger's and virtually cleared the shop out. Mr and Mrs Benger's daughter, Heather, was something of a glamour girl at the time, and, at some ten to twelve years older than me, an object of desire, but Mother was very protective of Heather.

Benger's shop

Paul Drinkwater (1949-1955)

Friends, past and present

I REMEMBER – sitting the 11-plus exam at Potterne School with Sheila Vooght, the village policeman's daughter, and Martin Broadbent, the Chief Fire Officer's son.

I remember – being interviewed at Potterne School by Miss Guy and Mr Lewis.

I remember – my parents receiving the letter offering me a place at the Grammar School.

At the swimming pool, summer 1955

I remember – going to Mr Kemp's shop in the Brittox to buy the school uniform. My mother had to buy it piece by piece, as it was quite expensive. When we had the complete uniform I remember visiting my grandparents to show it off.

I remember the first day at school. It was so different from village school life, having to move from class to class for each lesson, new subjects such as French and Science, wearing the uniform and remembering always to wear the beret when going into the town, walking from Bath Road to Southbroom for games.

I remember – swimming at the old swimming pool at Rotherstone. The pool was unheated so often the temperature was only 50-52 degrees. I had learnt to swim before going to the Grammar School as my uncle was Sid Dowse, the swimming pool Superintendent.

I remember – Tony Duck driving his MG sports car up the drive at Braeside, but we were not allowed to ride bicycles up the drive!

I remember – the Dramatic Society productions of *Merrie England* and and *The Mikado*, helping behind the scenes with wardrobe.

I remember – school dinners in the canteen, with the two sitting system. My favourite meal was spam fritters.

I remember – friends that I still see around Devizes – Mary, Averil, Jill, Pete, Ann and not forgetting those to whom we have already said goodbye – Janet Merson, Cynthia Green and Janet Cheeseman.

I remember – leaving school to work at David Owen's; Mr Lewis was very helpful in getting me the job.

I remember – the teachers, the school secretary, Miss Chivers and Mr John the Headmaster.

Looking back, I enjoyed my time at DGS, value the friends I made and still see at the reunions organised by Peter and Gordon Paget. The Grammar School gave me confidence, as I have never had a problem with speaking in public.

Jennifer Lake (née Burt 1949-1955)

God save the Queen!

SATURDAY FEBRUARY 2nd 1952 is a date well remembered in our family. It was the day that my sister Mary was born. She followed four brothers, all of whom attended the Grammar School and we were all very elated to have a young sister to complete the family.

Four days later on February 6th, our class was in the only classroom on the first floor, adjacent to the Science labs. We were eagerly awaiting the arrival of our Maths. Teacher, Tommy Watkins. He strolled purposefully into the room, saying that he had an announcement to make. 'The King is dead', he said with much solemnity, 'God save the Queen!' We were all stunned in our seats; this was devastating news.

One small boy in the front of the class raised a timorous hand. 'Yes, boy?' said T.E.W.

'Does that mean we will have a constipation, Sir?'

'Stupid boy', snapped our mentor, 'Coronation!'

My thoughts at the time were more personal. My sister Mary had lived in as many reigns as I had!

T.E.W. often recalled this story when we met at social functions. He had a great sense of humour and was well respected in the town. The small boy? That remains our little secret.

Peter Paget (1950-1955)

A twenty-two mile round journey and yesterday's cakes

MY FATHER was a Warrant Officer in the Royal Air Force based at Upavon. For the Spring term I attended Rushall Primary School, where my classmates could not comprehend that I had already lived in Yorkshire, Cheshire, London and Singapore. It was also a shock for me to learn that some of them had never even seen the sea.

The results of my taking the 11-plus at my London school came through and I was to attend Devizes Grammar School. But how was I to get there? It was eleven miles away and family cars were unheard of then. About eight of us travelled from the RAF camp by public service bus at 8.15 a.m. to the village, then caught another bus to Devizes, arriving in the Market Place at 9.05 a.m., then walked along the Bath Road to school, arriving after assembly and sometimes missing the beginning of the first lesson. Returning home was just as complicated and we were never back before 6 p.m. It did, however, give us the opportunity of buying 'yesterday's' cakes at the Pie Shop and doing our homework in rough or helping other people with their 'lines' on the homeward bus. Sometimes in the winter when the weather was really bad we did not even get to school because the bus drivers were not prepared to take the responsibility for getting us to Devizes, so we trudged back up the hill through the snow to enjoy a couple of days off. Unfortunately the distance form school and lack of suitable transport meant that we were unable to participate in some sporting, musical and dramatic activities which took place after school

Walking from one building to the other across the main road for different lessons did cause a few problems, and took some getting used to, as did walking through the town to the sports field, especially on market day when shoppers did not appreciate being confronted with young people carrying hockey sticks or football boots. Swimming lessons and sports took place at the nearby pool and I have memories of stiff blue fingers trying to get myself dressed again after the sessions.

The environment of the school was friendly and comfortable. Members of staff appeared to us to be strict but fair, and the freedom to move around the beautiful grounds of Braeside and play or watch tennis on the top lawn were highlights of the summer term. Some wonderful Shakespearian productions were staged in the open air theatre; because of transport problems I could not take part in these but I did help make some of the costumes and sets. I remember being in a History lesson with Miss Read when we heard that George VI had died, and one day the whole school congregated outside Braeside to view, very carefully, the eclipse of the sun. We also made a trip *en masse* to the local cinema to see *The Ascent of Everest*. I was in the school choir and under Mr Howells' leadership we were successful in the local Eisteddfods, held in the Corn Exchange. This was also the venue for the annual prize-giving days, when we all had to be on our best behaviour and in immaculate uniform, and came away feeling full of pride after singing the school song.

I only remained in the Sixth Form for one year and was always disappointed that I didn't join the select band of pupils who were allowed to use the prefects' lodge. Although I was not particularly academic and struggled in some subjects to keep up, especially Maths and Latin, the staff were always supportive, and looking back I realise that we were given a very good basic educational grounding, which stood us in good stead for the future. My memories of schooldays here are happy, basically trouble free and with an innocence which has been lost by the modern generation. Because numbers in the school were relatively low, it was easy to get to know people and a lot of us still retain those friendships to this day.

Pat Macey (née Williams 1951-1957)

Dancing and meteorology

SPORT WAS NOT REALLY my love at DGS and I well remember feeling relieved that acute appendicitis in the last week of the 1954 summer holidays kept me out of the Rugby XV, much to the chagrin of Mr Watkins, the PE master. Also having a dislike for football I was pleased to be able to train for the cross country during games lessons and this helped me to win the senior boys' race in 1958. Even more desirable was being able to play tennis in Hillworth Park in preference to cricket which I also disliked.

One of my most enduring memories of those schooldays was organising the Friday evening dancing club sessions. Dancing had become a real love of mine. Dancing club had been introduced by Miss Read in 1951 and was open to members of the Fifth and Sixth forms, who under her expert tuition soon became accomplished in the art of 'slow, slow, quick, quick, slow'. When she was no longer able to run the class herself, a rota of members of staff remained on the premises in the school hall, while I took over the tuition. Instruction was given in both Old Time and Modern Ballroom dancing and the evening was always a very popular end of the week diversion with the Fifth and Sixth forms. Then along came Rock'n'Roll and on one memorable Friday night when 'Rock around the Clock' was smuggled on to the turn table, I smashed it in disgust! Many romances blossomed at dancing club and the season always culminated with the much anticipated party at the end of the Spring term. In 1958, my last year as M.C., a small jazz band formed by the trumpet-playing French *assistant* M.Penso entertained the dancers during the interval of the party.

A more creative streak was the setting up of a meteorological station on the lawn at Braeside. My interest in Geography and Meteorology was to be the key to my success in finally getting to university and I have always been grateful to Mr Lewis, the Careers Master, who advised me to stick to horticulture, my other early love, and use my prowess in Geography to get into university rather than pursuing a career in meteorology – 'Your maths is not good enough' he said.

With Mr Heaward's encouragement I formed a meteorological society during my time in the Sixth form and as a result of a woodwork project, presided over by that 'gentle giant' Mr Burt, we constructed a weather station which in the autumn of 1957 took its place on Braeside lawn to register daily weather readings. A regular monthly weather synopsis became a feature in *the Devizes Gazette* until I left to go to Nottingham University in October 1958. I still have a climate station at my home in Christchurch, New Zealand and have taken 9 a.m. readings every day of my life for more years than I care to remember.

The weather station, mid 1950s

Robert Crowder (1951-1958)

Memories of Music and Drama at DGS

I STARTED at Devizes Grammar School in September 1951, a few days before my eleventh birthday. Because I had already been learning the violin for about two years, I was allowed to join the string orchestra in my first term, which was considered quite unusual. I remember how we used to take part in the Wiltshire Music Festival, competing against schools from other towns, then combining with them to play in the Friday afternoon concert. It seems extraordinary that Haydn Howells, who took all the music at the school and whose whole life in Devizes seemed to be involved with music, should have been appointed originally as games master at the school and then in later years taught Latin; in my day music was never offered at school for GCE or A- level. The orchestra used to perform at Open Days and I remember one year when I had to play my violin, dressed in costume and full make up as the king for 'The Princess and the Woodcutter', as there wasn't time to change between the two performances. The play was performed on the amphitheatre at Braeside, which previously had been the setting for productions of *Merrie England* in 1953, and *The Mikado* in 1954. I only ever had minor roles in the school plays but used to get a slip added to my school report, saying that I had taken part and performed with enthusiasm, signed by H.W.Haycock. One role that haunts me still was

The DGS string quartet. Graham Hancock (viola), David Pickering (cello), Eric Gilbert (violin), Michael Oliver (violin)

when I played the reindeer in *The Snow Queen*. For the first night performance the mask that I was to wear had not arrived and the head was made in school for me from *papier-maché* on a wire frame, but for the second performance and for the rest of the week I had to wear a mask made of rubber , the inside of which was extremely airless and after my few moments on stage I was almost in need of oxygen!

A highlight of the autumn term was the carol concert, on the Monday evening after the week of the play; I continued to be involved with it after I left school. Devizes Evening String Orchestra played for the carol singing, a tradition which continued after I took over as conductor from Haydn Howells in 1961. I can still remember how we had to play ' The Boar's Head Carol' before the interval

VIth form jazz band 1958. Christopher Wiltshire, Rhys Jones, Monsieur Penso, John Ayers, Graham Hancock

until everyone had gone out of the canteen , then follow them into B6 for refreshments, the choir continuing to sing the carol outside Braeside.

I left school in July 1958 after seven very happy years. It was only just over a year later that I was asked to teach violin and recorder there. I used the mobile hut by the side of the canal for lessons. I often felt as if I was on a boat, sailing along the canal. The form teacher for the class which used that room for registration was Daphne Broadway. She had always been able to fill me with a sense of terror when I was a pupil at the school and I remember one day, when I was packing away my instruments and music, that some of the pupils in that class were playing about and holding the door to prevent, as they thought, their friends getting in. Suddenly I heard Miss Broadway's voice, 'Who is holding that door?' It took a great deal of restraint to prevent myself saying, 'Not me Miss'. I continued to teach at the school until it amalgamated with Southbroom Secondary Modern School in 1969 and felt very privileged to have been invited to attend the last-ever end of term assembly in July and to enter the hall as a member of staff.

Michael Oliver (1951-1958)

Of Struggles and Strenuous Frays

'AS FOR YOU TWO, the way you're going, you'll be getting your marriage certificate before your School Certificate!' Thus my future wife and I were admonished by Mr Clook on finding us indulging in innocent hand holding in the 3A form room. There was something special about what today would be regarded as 'an item' at DGS in the fifties. As fifth formers we became used to Harry Haycock, at a play reading session saying, 'Pat, will you read Juliet?', his eyes pretending to roam over the class, 'Ah, yes, Wiltshire, will you read Romeo?' It was in Harry's lessons, though, that we both developed our love of poetry and prose, particularly the War Poets and the fashionable Thirties set, including Stephen Spender. 'What does the poet mean, Wiltshire, by feminine landscape?' I can imagine today's Eng.Lit. pupils responding 'shapely, sir, like a pair of boobs'. I seem to remember my response involved 'shapely' waving of my hands. Harry had a good ear for gossip and in reference to a smidgen of jealousy entering my life, I remember him murmuring, as he adjusted my wig for my improbable role of a swarthy Spaniard in *The Women have their Way*, 'Twixt Scylla and Charybdis are we?' I suppose it was one way of learning Greek legends. Harry's roots were, we presumed, northern (i.e. somewhere north of Swindon) and when ruffled, his accent could cut through his erstwhile gentle but precise pronunciation, as when Fishy Salmon was eating in class. 'Put it in the booket!' 'The what, sir?' 'The booket, boy, the booket!' roared Harry. 'Oh the bucket, sir, right sir'. On accents again, in my first effort at treading the boards, I played Kay in *The Snow Queen*. Near the end, after I had ridden back on a reindeer, I had the line, 'It was a fine ride', which inevitably came out as 'foine roid'. Harry sat there at rehearsal for fifteen minutes repeating 'fine ride' while I parroted back to him 'foine roid'. I think we settled on 'lovely journey'.

If these recollections seem centred on one personality, I make no apology. Harry was an inspiration to us (not that we recognised it at the time) and Pat would claim that her upper second in English, which she completed as a mature student, had its origins in those formative lessons. But we also both owed a great deal to 'Killer' Howells. He it was who asked me to accompany the school choir, (as Pat was a member, this seemed an excellent idea) and also to conduct the madrigal group, thus leaving him free to become the only tenor. Pat's love of choral singing was born at school and has become a life-long passion; witness her thirty years as a first soprano in the acclaimed Sheffield Philharmonic chorus. Howells also taught us Latin, and again, though I was not to appreciate it for some years, that grounding in what is the most glorious language in which to sing, served Pat and me well throughout our musical lives. As regards his performances, who could forget 'Killer' Nanki-Pooing his way through *The Mikado*, dressed in *green* tights, so that as he moved across the grass of the open-air theatre at Braeside, his voice seemed to emanate from a floating torso.

Then, of course, there was Tommy Watkins whom I once threw to the floor in a practice rugby match. My reward for this 'bravery' was to be put in the school XV as full back. 'Wiltshire's not afraid to tackle,' he insisted to the Spacey brothers who, also being Welsh, dominated rugby in the school. I don't think they were convinced. And as the forwards from Swindon Commonweal bore down on me and the ball on a cold, wet, muddy Saturday morning, I regretted that foolhardy display at Southbroom.

There seemed to be a good number of teachers with the nickname 'Daddy' – 'Daddy' Burt looking at the lathe and the chunk of wood that some hapless pupil was trying to shape into a slender lamp standard- 'And what have we here? – a rain water butt?' Then there was lovely 'Daddy' Dunn, who should never have had us inflicted on him, he was so talented and gentle, and 'Daddy' Moore with his easily forgettable efforts to impress on us the finer points of Biology. From Form 1J one remembers Mrs Jones with her joke about the Frenchman who has had sufficient breakfast if he has had an egg. I think this failed to awaken an interest in *l'entente cordiale* but somehow Mademoiselle Ausina *was* able to produce a Gallic flicker in the boys. Miss Broadway must have had a hand in Pat's culinary expertise, from which I have benefited all my life. Millie Guy and 'Lump' Lewis, (he, the smooth quick stepper), along with Headmaster Denys John, tried to persuade my parents against letting me take up music –'Does Christopher know what a very precarious career it is?' said John, 'after all Beethoven died a pauper'. None could forget the delectable Miss Read, who set the testosterone racing in every lad in the school from the third form upwards. I even understood the significance of 'Prehistory ' and 'History', the first words she wrote on the blackboard in lesson one, so attentive was I to her discourse.

Devizes Grammar School Song

Our School we sing and its noble height
With its front to the northern breeze
Its spacious halls and its aspect bright
And the green encircling trees
We sing of the joy of Girl and Boy
Of struggles and strenuous frays
Of comrades dear and our friends so near
Of those bright and happy days
Then Hurrah for the D.G.S.
May its honour and fame increase
Then Hurrah with a right goodwill
For the school on the crest of the hill

As a musician, I must admit that my one disappointment in terms of staff at DGS brings me back to 'Killer' Howells (or 'Ego' as he was known to earlier generations). I only had one year in the sixth form, but during that time 'Killer' approached me about composing a new school song – 'not the words you understand, we couldn't possibly change those'. In his efforts not to offend the lyricist, who perhaps was then still alive, he had missed the point that it was precisely the ghastly doggerel that needed to be condemned to oblivion as well as the mundane melody. However, I came up with a Waltonesque march that had a singable line and vaguely contemporary progressions. But Howells never got round to teaching it. Therefore, like any decent jobbing composer, I had to find a use for the piece. And so it became the Wedding March when Pat and I got married in 1962. Thus it was performed once and once only.

'So Hurrah, with a right good will, For the school on the crest of the hill' – see what I mean?

Christopher Wiltshire (1952-1958)

Sporting Memories

I BECAME A PUPIL at the school in September 1952, Wartime rationing was still lingering, the country had returned Winston Churchill as Prime Minister and Newcastle United were FA Cup holders for the second year in succession.

After suffering the indignity of the ritual 'banking' ceremony, I was soon participating in the break time football 'knockabouts'. Nobody owned a proper football in those austere times so we made do with a tennis ball and used the sides of the Art room as an improvised goal. My early soccer skills probably owed more to these sessions than the curriculum games lessons. At the end of the school day, most of the school trooped up to the Market Place to catch their buses back to the local villages, while those fortunate enough to live in the town lingered on the premises to play 'fives' on the courts at the back of the school. We either played the game with gloved hands or with plywood bats crafted in Mr Burt's adjacent woodwork room. It was a good grounding for squash and tennis in later years. Being soccer mad, it came as something of a shock to me to have to play rugby in our first term, a game that was entirely alien to all of my year at first, but it was the passion of our short-tempered Welsh PE and Maths teacher, Mr Watkins, who in those early years used to scare me to death!

Games lessons, time tabled one afternoon a week, involved a mile long trek or bike ride to the Southbroom playing fields, but living in the town, I was allowed to go home to change, thus avoiding the cramped and draughty wooden games pavilion, with its cold showers (not much fun for visiting teams on Saturdays either!). PE lessons took place twice a week in the school hall, hemmed in by classrooms on three sides and a small stage by the entrance. We changed in the cloakroom and tussled to sit on the central heating pipes in winter. There were limitations as to how thirty boys could exercise in such a confined space, but I recall that we did a lot of 'Swedish' drill and medicine ball games in four straight lines, gymnastics with a partner, rope climbing and vaulting over a sectioned box and buck. If it wasn't freezing cold, teams would go outside to play an unsupervised game of basket ball, using the girls' netball posts. We wore white T shirts and shorts and had to have our house colour sewn on to the seams of our shorts – blue for St. Andrew's, red for St. George's and yellow for St. David's.

Devizes was fortunate to have a fine outdoor swimming pool just up the road in Rotherstone. In the summer term one PE lesson a week was devoted to swimming, whatever the water temperature. Sid Dowse, the pool Superintendent, had taught me to swim in 1951 and many enjoyable hours were spent there during the infrequent spells of hot weather in the mid '50s. The sun always seemed to shine for the school swimming gala, held in the morning in the last week of the summer term, with the whole school watching from the tiered

Swimming sports winners 1955. Back row (left to right): Lesley Elliott, Julia Macartney, Nellie Hawkins, Robert Crowder, Paul Pickering, Rhys Jones, Tony Hobbs, John Briody, Keith Parsons; Front row: Sylvia Cookman, Clifford Woodruffe, Gillian Child, Peter Baker, Beryl Bartlett, Valerie Nash, Graham Hancock, Lester Northeast, Veronica Banwell ?

concrete terracing. The nervous anticipation before the first event and the perfectly still blue water are indelibly etched into the memory.

DGS had regular Saturday sports fixtures in the 1950s – Autumn term – rugby, Spring term – soccer, and cricket in the Summer term. We played most of the grammar schools in the county and we usually managed to hold our own against schools of similar size, but were considerably disadvantaged against the likes of Trowbridge Boys' High and the two large Swindon grammar schools, Commonweal and Headlands. As they had much larger sixth form numbers to choose from, we were regularly trounced and it wasn't until my last year in 1960 that we won every soccer match on the fixture card and finally avenged the many losses in the previous decades.

One advantage of being in a school with a small sixth form was ' the large fish in a small pond' factor and if you showed any particular sporting talent you were 'blooded' (often 'bloodied') in the first team at quite a tender age. I made my début in the rugby team when I was in the fourth year, considerably undersized but fleet of foot, which was a useful attribute on the odd occasions the ball reached me on the wing! I can recall playing in a particular Saturday match alongside one of the prefects, only to be reprimanded by him for some misdemeanour the following Monday!

Athletic Sports winners 1957

DGS football team 1957. Back row (left to right): Graham Hancock, Roland Romain, Leslie Minty, Christopher Collett, Roger Butler, Colin Lampard, David Burt; Front row: Maurice Lovelock, David Osland, Michael Lee, Colin Megraw, Michael Miller

DGS rugby XV 1956. Back row (left to right): Mr Grimsley, Michael Lee, Clyde King, Christopher Wiltshire, Cyril Gaiger, Maurice Thorne, Keith Spacey, Rhys Jones, Bernard Robbins, Robert Crowder, Michael Pitcher, Mr Beasley; Front row: Colin Megraw, Graham Hancock, Mr Watkins, Richard Perkins, Peter Spacey, Leslie Minty, Tony Hobbs; Front: David Burt, Joe Peare

Athletics played a prominent part in my school sporting career. The area sports at Southbroom before Whitsun were followed by the county sports, the venue for which moved around Wiltshire each year. Probably my most outstanding year was 1959 when I represented Wiltshire at the All England Schools Championships at Northwich and reached the semi-final of the under-19 hundred yards. The school inter-house sports were held at Southbroom in the summer term, and no matter what date was selected, proceedings always seemed to be interrupted by rain or showers; in fact the 1957 event had to be abandoned, to be completed the following day. Records were set and broken over the years and there were junior champions, middle school champions and in the senior department *Victor* and *Victrix Ludorum*

No sporting memoir would be complete without mentioning the annual cross-country race at the end of the Spring term, which in theory was compulsory for all boys from the second form upwards, but in reality was often avoided by the 'sick, lame and lazy' on the slender evidence of a dubious note from home. If you were keen you trained for the race in PE lessons and if you were serious about winning you went out running in the evenings. Starting in the fields below the Braeside woods, there would be a mad dash to be the first to reach the stile, and then on to Conscience Lane via Iron Pear Tree Farm. At the Roundway House gates, the junior race took the shorter two and a half mile route through the grounds, while the seniors negotiated the longer hilly road section to Roundway village. Joining up with the junior course was a stony field track and both races proceeded down Quaker's Walk and thence along the canal towpath to the Nursery on the Bath Road, and finally on to the lawn at Braeside, where a trilby-hatted Mr Howells would hand out the positions to the exhausted finishers. For me, pain would usually set in along Quaker's Walk, and then if I was up among the leaders it was a case of hanging on in there until the finish. Perhaps one enduring memory of the cross-country was being a member of the team that beat Bishop Wordsworth's

Graham Hancock winning the junior cross-country 1955

School from Salisbury in a one-off inter-school match in 1957. Surprisingly, nearly fifty years on, it would still be possible to run around the entire senior course, if the spirit and flesh were willing!

In retrospect, I experienced some very happy years at DGS and I owe much to the dedication and encouragement of the teaching staff, in particular Mr Watkins and Mr Lewis, who helped me to gain a place at Loughborough College of Physical Education, leading to a rewarding thirty-two year career in teaching.

Graham Hancock (1952-1960)

D.G.S. . . . . . a Different Grammar School

WHEN I MOVED to Devizes in September 1953, I thought I knew all about Grammar Schools as I had already been attending one for three years. I knew that Grammar Schools were large buildings with long corridors where pupils walked in single file in silence, always keeping to the left, when moving from one class to another. Grammar Schools were not exactly prisons, but it was unheard of to leave the school premises during school hours, and eating sweets was strictly forbidden.

Obviously, none of this was true of D.G.S. and I was completely confused at first. I started in 4B and found it very strange to walk through one classroom to get to another. Changing rooms between lessons was another bewildering experience. In the entrance hall at Braeside there was movement in all directions at the same time, and it could be quite noisy. People were even going up and down the same staircase at the same time! At my previous school there had been certain stairs for going up and others for coming down. Moving between buildings and walking to the other side of the town for games lessons were other routines that made D.G.S. different. What was even more surprising was that during the dinner hour we were allowed to cross the road to the sweet shop and then, back in the school grounds, eat the sweets we had bought!

I still have vivid memories of some of the first lessons I had at D.G.S. In Maths. Mr.Lewis asked me something. I didn't hear the question properly, but thought I should answer 'yes'. Then I was surprised when everyone including Mr. Lewis laughed. He had actually asked me if I could do Maths. When we had our first Geography lesson we were told that we would be learning about Asia that term. I thought that was rather boring as it was what I had done in the third year in my other school. Then Mr. Clook wanted to know if I had lived in Singapore. My father was in the army so that was a possibility, but I hadn't. Mr. Clook then remarked that we were the only class in the school with no pupil who had lived in Singapore.

At the end of my first term, I was moved into the other class which was a bit unsettling, but not such a big change as starting at D.G.S. I soon got used to the new class and the rest of my four years at D.G.S. were very happy. Some of my memories are like snapshots. I remember Miss Guy teaching us clause analysis. Most of us seemed to have great difficulty in understanding all the different adverbial clauses of manner. Then in History lessons we had to write many notes very quickly. I sat at the very end of a row next to a girl who was left handed. As I am right handed our arms were often bumping, and we got a bit annoyed with each other. It was nearly fifty years after we left school and met again that we realised how easy the solution to that problem was. We should have just changed places! I had never experienced a Harvest Festival in school before I moved to Devizes, but that was nothing to the surprise I had when we had to sing 'While Shepherds watched their flocks by night' to the tune of 'On Ikla Moor ba tat' at Christmas. Christmas parties were special at D.G.S. too. I can't even remember having parties at any other school I attended.

There are pleasant memories of the summer terms also. I remember sitting in the sun at the back of Braeside watching tennis. It might have been the finals of the tennis tournament. Then there was the open air theatre. That was certainly something that made D.G.S. different. I remember seeing *The Mikado* there. That was my introduction to Gilbert and Sullivan and it is still my favourite. Another summer memory is the delicious fresh fruit ice cream made by Mrs. Benger.

At D.G.S. we were really lucky when we reached the Sixth Form as our classes were so small. I remember French lessons in Mr. John's study, when he brought along some of the very latest technology to help us. I don't think any of us had seen a tape recorder before.

D.G.S. was unique. There were many things it lacked. There were no playing fields close to the school, there were no modern science labs and the library was very small. Braeside was not an ideal building for a school. But these things did not matter, as there was a friendly atmosphere and we were helped and encouraged to do our best. I am glad I went to Devizes Grammar School. My only regret is that I was only there for four years and not seven.

Georgina Tay (née Sayer 1953-57)

Gold out of clay

IN SEPTEMBER 1953 I waited at Bishops Cannings for the bus to take me to my first day at Devizes Grammar School. I was placed in Mrs Jones's form in the classroom to the side of the hall. Mrs Jones was a kindly lady, coming up to retirement. She wore a big skirt and always carried a big handbag which was full of work to be marked. She had a twinkle in her eye and I have often recalled her saying to us in Religious Instruction, 'Why are missionaries like prunes? Because they go into the dark interior and do good work!' It always gets a laugh! She gave us our time table worked out by the Senior Master, Mr Lewis and handed out text books which had to be named, and repaired if necessary with a covering of brown paper. Some of these books were up to ten years old. I remember my first break time because I was 'banked' as was the tradition.

Looking back fifty years I remember very little disruption in class as the teachers were mostly in control. School rules were respected and prefects had a lot of responsibility. We had a wide choice of subjects and this enabled me later to gain entrance to veterinary college. In sport we had fixtures with other schools and there was keen rivalry between the houses in athletics, swimming, cross-country and tennis. It enabled those with a special talent to shine, such as David Othen scoring a century at cricket, Graham Hancock winning the hundred yards, Anthony Hobbs the half mile and Clive Wordley throwing the javelin at All-England level. The school orchestra and choir also gave an opportunity for those with ability, such as Chris Wiltshire on the piano. Competitions, too, provide another opening for achievement; I won the verse speaking competition twice and can still remember the poems.

But the most important activity for me was the Dramatic Society. Mr Haycock's direction was very special; he made gold out of clay and brought love of the theatre to many. So much was achieved on the tiny canteen stage. On the night of the play, being adorned with make-up and dressing up in the costume made for an electric atmosphere, never to be forgotten. Mr Haycock also took us on theatre visits, to the Old Vic and Stratford.

Enjoying the grounds at Braeside. Left to right: Pat Stephenson, Jean Gleeson, Valerie James, Pauline Jones, Muriel Hall, Pamela Lye

All in all, we were very lucky in our teachers and our surroundings. The lawn, gardens and woods made for a pleasant background to our education, and although at times the library and classrooms became over-crowded, I look back on my school years with gratitude and affection.

Alan Carter (1953-1960)

The Golden Jubilee Celebrations 1956

DURING THE WEEKEND of July 27-29, 1956, the Golden Jubilee of DGS was celebrated at the main school building and at Braeside. Pat Kennedy, the Secretary of the Old Students' Association, was successful in tracing forty-one of the original 96 students and ten were able to attend part or all of the celebrations. The number on the school roll had grown to 348 by 1956 and a total of 3,066 students had passed through the school in the fifty years. The Headmaster of the time was Denys John and two surviving headmasters were able to attend the comprehensive programme arranged by a committee of sixteen.

Friday 27th saw an Open Day, with various exhibitions of school work and a museum of school history and achievements, which was open for the whole weekend. Among the exhibits was the renowned bicycle and bag of 'Froggy' Lund. Apparently he rode the same bicycle to school for thirty-one years. Numerous photographs and other memorabilia were there, including class and team photographs, school caps and uniform and memories of school trips abroad. A display of italic handwriting, a technique that had been introduced to the school by Mr John, was also mounted by Ann Giddings and Alan Carter, both of whom had won national success in this field. Mr Haycock and Miss Read gave demonstrations of stage make-up, an art they used to good effect in all the school plays they produced. The Open Day was followed by a concert at the open-air theatre. In the evening a celebration dinner was held at *The Castle Hotel* for which tickets were twelve shillings each. On Saturday 28 July a reception and 'At Home' were held at Braeside, followed by an informal party with Mr Lewis as Master of Ceremonies. Pioneer students and staff present included Miss Lois Eden, Miss E E Float, Miss A B Paradise, Miss A L Fisher, Miss Buchan-Sydeserff, Mr A H Rose and Colonel C F Linnett. One millionaire came to light – James Edwards who had become a businessman in Illinois. Invention also featured with F. George, who had developed and patented a machine to bottle milk and put the bottles into crates. On Sunday 29 July there was a religious service conducted by the Rev. Alwyn Jones, who was not only a former student but also the son of two members of staff. The first lesson was read by Roy Kemp, a former pupil and later Chairman of the Board of Governors of the school.

One highlight of the Jubilee was the collection of funds by the Old Students' Association for the provision of a new pair of gates for Braeside. One bore a bronze plaque with the borough arms, the other a similar plaque inscribed with the reasons for its presentation. These were officially opened in 1957 by Miss Float, a former Senior Mistress at the school. Despite the demise of DGS and the various subsequent uses for Braeside, the gates remain in place as a permanent reminder of very happy days spent there and in the prefects' lodge, which sadly has not survived. This refuge for prefects boasted a coal fire on which numerous pieces of toast were made during free periods. It was akin to the prefects having their own little rest room-cum-dining facility.

Jim Smith (1946-1954)

A culture shock

I CAME to Devizes Grammar School from Headlands Grammar School in Swindon. Headlands was very authoritarian, with strict discipline – you even got detention for speaking in the corridors or during assembly. DGS was quite a culture shock – my very first lesson was English Literature with Mr Haycock and pupils actually laughed in his class!

As a late-comer I found it difficult to be accepted at first and had to suffer a certain amount of ragging both about my surname and about the angle I wore my beret. Because of this (at least I hope so) I was often called 'pancake'. I was soon taken under the wing of Marianne Baker and am still friendly with her today.

School dinners were rather different from the meals served to schoolchildren today. In the dining room adjoining Braeside we sat at tables for six or eight and were supervised by the teachers who sat on a raised dais at one end of the room. We took our turn, table by table, to queue up to be served by the cooks. Maggie Ward and I would eat almost anything the others on the table did not want!

There were many extra-curricular activities. Choral verse speaking was taught by Mrs John, and we used to meet at the Johns' house in Stanley Terrace. We even went up to Friends House in London once and competed against some very swanky private schools. I believe we came second in our group despite mispronouncing a name in one of the poems. I still remember 'Sand in the sandwiches, wasps in the tea' and 'Where the waters of Eridamus run' and this is nearly 50 years ago! The calligraphy classes have shaped my handwriting even today but I remember being very jealous of the beautiful handwriting of Barbara Young. Other events which gave great pleasure were the choirs and the Eisteddfods. After the competition there would be a massed choir concert in the Corn Exchange. At Christmas there was the carol concert held in the dining hall. Afterwards we would parade to Braeside and, making an archway over the door, sing 'The Boars Head in hand bear I' as the audience trooped through to the house for a special Christmas buffet prepared by Miss Broadway. It was a truly magical evening for me.

I never won a prize but I do remember one occasion when the then mayor of Devizes gave out the prizes. I shall never forget what he said; 'I 'opes as the Queen and 'er 'usband 'as an 'appy 'omecoming'. There was much unkind merriment afterwards.

I hated games and used any excuse to get out of them. Why did I hate them? They were boring – there were always too many for the hockey team and Nancy Hehir and I used to get stuck in goal. We would entertain ourselves by hanging from the goalposts and making monkey noises and gestures. After this came the dreaded showers. There was little privacy and we never had time to get properly dry and had to drag on our clothes whilst still quite damp. I still dislike showers. For chemistry we were grouped in twos or threes when conducting experiments. This proved to be a problem as none of us (myself, Barbara Young and Michael Oliver) liked lighting the Bunsen burners; I was always afraid they would explode. I loved art and even enjoyed cleaning out the drains when they got blocked with paint. I can also remember clearing a drain in domestic science when someone disposed of their excess pastry by flushing it down the sink. Doing this is one of my happiest memories of domestic science as I was terrified of Miss Broadway to the extent that I asked to be allowed to do extra maths instead of domestic science. Later, however, I found out that Miss Broadway could be extremely kind if you were ill and had to visit the sickroom.

Mr Clook was another of my bugbears. He had been a fighter pilot in the war and after an accident had a metal plate inserted in his skull. When Mr Clook had a headache the headmaster, Mr John, used to come into class and remind us of this and tell us to be well behaved. Looking back on it now, I think I was a little unkind to him but he wasn't very nice to us girls. As for most of the other teachers, I either respected them (some could appear a little severe) or liked them. Miss Myfanwy Davies was renowned for her jewellery, Miss Read was a fashion icon – her dress of the day was regularly observed and discussed. Mr Moore, Mr Howells and Mr. Burt always seemed kind and I remember them with affection.

FRIDAY, 27TH JULY.

2-0 p.m.   Open Day.
to   Main School Building, Bath Road.
4-0 p.m.

Room 1
Exhibition and Museum of School History and Achievements.

Art Room
Exhibition of Arts and Crafts.

Chemistry, Biology and Physics Laboratories
Exhibitions and Displays.

Domestic Science Kitchen
Exhibition of Work.

Woodwork Room
Exhibition of Work.

2-30 p.m.   *Main School Field*
P.T. Display by Girls.

Braeside :
History Room
Dramatic Society Exhibition.

Geography Room
Geography Exhibition.

3-30 p.m.   *Open Air Theatre*
Concert by School Choirs and Orchestra.

7-0 p.m.   Old Students' Association Dinner.
for   Castle Hotel.
7-30 p.m.   Chairman : The Headmaster.
Informal Dress. Closing date for obtaining tickets from the Hon. Secretary of the O.S.A., Friday, 20th July.

SATURDAY, 28TH JULY.

2-30 p.m.   Reception at "Braeside."
to   Afterwards " At Home " :
4-30 p.m.
Miss Lois Eden, Mr. E. S. Roberts, Mr. H. F. Halliwell, Mr. D. W. John, Miss E. E. Float, Miss A. B. Paradise, Miss A. L. Fisher, Miss M. Buchan-Sydserff, Miss R. E. Guy, Mrs. E. G. Jones, Col. C. F. Linnitt, Mr. A. F. Lund, Mr. H. T. Lewis.

7-30 p.m.   An Informal Party.
to   School Hall.
11-0 p.m.   (Staff, Ex-Staff, Old Students, Vth and VIth Forms).
Master of Ceremonies : H. T. Lewis, Esq.

SUNDAY, 29TH JULY.

2-30 p.m.   Religious Service.
School Hall.
(Staff, Ex-Staff, Old Students, Vth and VIth Forms).
Conducted by the Rev. Alwyn Jones.

The O.S.A. Exhibition will be open each afternoon throughout the weekend.

Jubilee programme 1956

OSA golden jubilee reunion dinner 1956. Left to right. Mr H N White, Mrs O M Giles, Mr C S Sainsbury, Mr D W John, Miss E L Smart, Mr A E Stephenson, Miss L E Hinxman

Presentation of the Jubilee gates, funded by the Old Students' Association, October 1957. Left to right: Mr Oram, Chairman of the Governors, Miss Float, Mr D W John and Miss Fisher

Menu	Toasts
Cream of Tomato Soup	THE QUEEN *Proposed by* The Chairman
Roast Turkey Game Chips Fresh Peas New Potatoes	THE PIONEERS *Proposed by* Prefect, David Pickering *Responders* Miss Lily Hinxman Mr. Harvey White
Fruit Salad Vanilla Ice	THE FIFTY YEARS' TRADITION *Proposed by* Lieut.-Col. C. F. Linnitt *Responder* Mr. Harold Poole
Biscuits and Cheese	
Coffee	THE CHAIRMAN *Proposed by* Mr. Clifford Morgan

OSA golden jubilee reunion dinner 1956, dinner menu

Miss Guy and Mr Howells were a little distant but always fair. At first I was a little afraid of Mr Lewis but once I got to know him I found him an extremely kind person and he even helped me pass my 'O' level maths after I left school. He would give me lessons at his house.

VIth form fancy dress party 1957

Staff group outside Braeside 1958

I remember my last year at DGS as one of the happiest. I had a great group of friends – Nancy Hehir, Maggie Ward, Barbara Young, Heather Strange and Ann Daniels. It was a great wrench when I had to leave at the end of the 5th form but my father was not a great believer in education for girls and he felt it was time I started to earn my living.

Barbara Fuller (née Bobby, 1954-1956)

Caesar's Gallic Wars, railway tea and cigarette boxes

IN PEWSEY we had the option of Marlborough or Devizes Grammar School. I opted for DGS because my cousins and most of my friends were going there. The daily journey from my home in Pewsey was by Wilts and Dorset double decker bus, which picked up at *The Crown* in Wilcot Road at 7.45 a.m. The journey was then via Wilcot, Manningford, Woodborough, Bottlesford, Hilcott, Beechingstoke, Patney, All Cannings, Etchilhampton and then Devizes. On the morning run it took us to the school gates, but in the afternoon we walked into town to catch the bus outside *The Market Tavern*. The journey took an hour each way. I remember learning my Latin translations of Caesar's *Gallic Wars* and Virgil's *Aeneid* by heart by constant re-reading on the bus. If the weather was impossible for the bus to get through after deep snow, or the toppling of

Braeside in summer

Male prefects outside the prefects' lodge 1959. Back row (left to right): Alan J Carter, Edward Bowden, Frank Hayward, Richard Taylor, Michael Pitcher, Nicholas Gregson, Alan P Carter; Front row: Graham Hancock, Paul Salmon

trees across the road after strong gales, we caught a train; I can't remember whether we had to pay or not. I preferred this way of travel, especially if my father was on duty as signalman at Patney and Chirton Junction station. Then, whilst my classmates shivered on a cold platform waiting for the Devizes train, I could trot down to the signal box for a quick mug of 'railway tea' with Dad.

For several years we used to save a seat if the bus was crowded for Mrs Simms, who got on at Etchilhampton. We would double up and sit on each other's laps so that she could have a seat. We didn't do it for anyone else! At the end of each term we would ride our bikes to school and then go back to Mrs Simms at Etchilhampton for tea. I kept up that friendship with occasional letters and Christmas cards until Mrs Simms died.

I remember that the gardens and grounds at Braeside were kept to a high standard by the groundsmen and caretaker. We had the freedom of the grounds at break time. Working under 'Daddy' Burt, we made twenty different models, embracing various woodworking techniques and joints. One of the later models was a cigarette box. Little did 'Daddy' Burt know that several of these cigarette boxes found a resting place in the wooded bank at the bottom of the Braeside lawn. The inveterate smokers amongst us would keep a secret supply of cigarettes there and rush down each break time for a surreptitious 'puff'.

I felt quite honoured to be made a school prefect in my final sixth form year. Using the lodge at the bottom of the drive was a privilege and much sought after! Dancing Club on Friday nights was much anticipated and a number of boy–girl friendships started there and some led to long and successful marriages. I did not really appreciate, until I became a teacher myself some years later, how much we owed to those staff members who, at the end of a hard week, gave up their Friday evenings for our benefit.

Richard Giles (1955-1962)

High jinks on the last day of term 1960. Owner of A30 car an unknown member of staff. Left to right: David Othen, Michael Pitcher, David Osland, Graham Hancock, Andrew Stanton

A five-button cardigan and symmetrical potatoes

I HAVE BEEN THINKING of my time at school, and although it was a long time ago, it must have been a very positive experience as I remember it so fondly. I have spent my whole career as a teacher so I have had many opportunities to draw comparisons between DGS and the rest of the world.

Even though I enjoyed school, I was the same as all children in that I never wanted to give up the freedom of the summer holidays to start a new year. Slopers, the big department store in the Brittox, always changed their window display in August to include blackboard and easel with the sign 'Back to School' boldly printed on it. We tried to drag Mum away but she always needed to check the supply of uniform items. I expect we looked all right in our blazers, skirts, shirts and ties. I didn't think that tying a tie was difficult till I grew up and found people who hadn't tied one every day for years. I remember cycling to school in my gabardine raincoat, soaked to the skin; they were never were great in the wet. I did get into trouble when my mother knitted a navy cardigan for me, but she made it a button to the neck style, not a v-neck, 5-button version required by the uniform list. Miss Guy had something to say about that, so I spent that winter warmer but out of line by uniform standards. Those Clark's sandals! We all wore them so we did not object. How compliant we were compared to today's children! I cycled to school and had to go via New Park Street or through the Market Place, either way passing Wadworth's Brewery. I hated the smell of the malting process, so on days when that wafted freely, I inhaled deeply, head down and tried to cycle as far as I could without having to breathe that smell again.

As always, some teachers and subjects stay with us. Miss Broadway frightened us to death when we were young. I remember my first cookery attempts. Blancmange! How could it go wrong? But of course it did. We had to make potato and cheese pie next and went home with a list of ingredients, asking for potatoes all the same size. I remember my mother saying how could she manage if she could only use matching potatoes, but she sent me off with those required. At the end of cookery lessons we had to scrub the unvarnished wooden tables, wash the tea towels and hang them in a large biscuit tin-like gas drier. How antiquated it all seems today! I have taught Domestic Science for a year, although it is now called ' Design Technology' and it is so totally different as to be hardly recognisable as the same subject.

As we grew older we came to realise that Miss Broadway was delightful. Who else would stay late at school to watch the cooking Christmas cakes as they took their time to be ready? It was from her that I learned how to do fancy icing, enabling me later to ice my own wedding cake. Ann Ware and I went to visit Daphne after she retired, in fact not long before she died; she was still charming.

We privately referred to Mr Haycock as 'Harry'. I was captivated by English after his dynamic presentations in class. I fell in love with Dickens because he gave it such a flair. I took A level English where we studied *Bleak House*, not an easy read but I loved it. I don't think I would have been to Stratford without the school trips; they were very special and worthwhile. We even went to Marlborough College one year to see their production of *The Tempest*. I think my future enthusiasm for the theatre came from these experiences, besides the school productions, which were fantastic! I worked on make-up and loved the whole atmosphere of the productions, despite that awful canteen which had no theatrical ambience at all and probably smelled of old cabbage.

Miss Read's History classes were such fun. She managed to make history full of colour and such detail. I remember the Industrial Revolution as if it were yesterday. In fact I have taught that period of History myself and I hope I added as much sparkle as she did to us. Some subjects were not for me – Maths was one! My mother attended a parent-teacher interview where the master in question said, 'Mrs Smith, some children have mathematical ability and some don't. Hilary doesn't have it!' Nothing like a blunt put down, so I have lived up to his prediction. He didn't say, however, that I might have other talents.

DGS was the sort of school which kept the same staff for years. Devizes was a good place to live and I presume the school enjoyable to teach in. Mrs Jones and Miss Guy were there when I started and they had taught my father years before. I am sure that happened often with families who had been in the town for generations.

Miss Harmsworth, later Mrs Luckett, was perhaps the first person to harness my love of PE and all things physical. I had been a dance fanatic since the age of three, so this helped develop the idea of teaching PE as a career. Miss Loxton came next into the PE department, but her enthusiasm was lukewarm. It was finally the soft-spoken Mrs Davis who told me about PE colleges and made some recommendations. Mr Watkins pooh-poohed the idea of a girl going into the profession, but I was not deterred, and PE has taken me around the world and has been a great choice for me. If I think back to the meagre PE facilities we had, the multi-use hall, opening on to classrooms, a general walkway for everyone and very little equipment, it must have been difficult for the PE staff. I remember the walk to the swimming pool at Rotherstone, the even longer walk to Southbroom playing fields, but most of us arrived on time to change in the wooden pavilion. I am sure a bus would be required to transport everyone to and fro today. We did a fair bit of walking between Braeside and the old school. Some time must have been lost in transit but I don't remember being deliberately late.

I have been thinking about the influence a school in a small town such as DGS has upon its students. I loved film society and dance club, the drama productions and all the after school activities. These all helped to shape my love of the theatre and all things cultural. Much of this would have passed me by without those early introductions. I remember the Harvest Festival, with the tradition of having a flower-filled cross on the velvet curtains behind the small platform in the hall; sports days at the pool and the playing fields and prize giving in the Corn Exchange. If all of these events are still clear in my mind they must have been well run and enjoyable occasions.

We held the staff in some respect and fear. We didn't knock on the staff room door at break times unless we really had to. I was always struck by the smoke cloud which hung in the air when the door was opened. Did everyone smoke? Finally when I turned out my father's home recently, I found my old school reports. Everything was said as briefly as possible, but it seemed we were summed up pretty well, and parents and teachers were satisfied with this. I have been teaching recently and writing reports where each one is more like a book and not noticeably more helpful to parents.

Daphne Broadway and Elsie Greenwood

Hilary Hunt (née Smith 1955-1962)

A widening of horizons

MY MEMORIES of DGS are all very positive. I have often recalled my time there with affection. I recall superb English lessons with Mr Haycock. He also organised many trips to the theatre, including the Memorial Theatre at Stratford-on-Avon and the Oxford Playhouse. Having been a teacher myself, I now appreciate the hard work and the loss of personal free time involved in organising these visits. Mr Daines' economic history lessons gave me a lasting interest in the subject and I went on to read History at university. I always felt grateful to him for kindling my interest in the subject. I recall also an enjoyable holiday in Germany and Belgium, organised and led by Miss Thomas and Mr Dexter. Helping with costumes for Dramatic Society productions, such as *Cradle Song* and *Jonah and the Whale* also has happy associations. I look back on my

DGS at the Lycée de Grenoble, August 1961, led by Miss Thomas and Mr Dexter

time at DGS with happy memories of friends, teachers, my late parents and the beautiful Wiltshire countryside.

Diana Travers (née Bond 1957-1964)

'Daddy' Burt

I DID NOT GO to the Grammar School as a pupil, as I went to St.Peter's School in the next building, but we senior boys were allowed to attend the Grammar School for woodwork on a Friday afternoon for teaching by Mr Burt, who always wore a white apron. He was a very kind man with a fatherly manner which earned him his nickname. At the rear section of the woodwork shop, housed in an outbuilding, were a couple of metal turning lathes and a pillar drill. A corridor running at right angles housed the wood turning lathes, separating machines from hand tools, apart from 'Daddy' Burt's large circular wood saw which no one would dare to go near, as this was strictly out of bounds.

One of the first wood turning projects for the boys was to make a three-legged stool with three turned spindles for legs and a round top. It was always a challenge as to who could create the most turned grooves in their top. But no one took the advice of 'Daddy' Burt that the more grooves you made the more uncomfortable it was to sit on !

Boys will be boys and the usual schoolboy pranks and rituals went on. When a boy was new to the woodwork class he was subjected to an initiation rite, which involved putting a handful of sawdust in the back end of a blower contraption, which 'Daddy' had ingeniously created to clean off the lathes. The blowing end of the pipe was pushed up the trouser leg of the newcomer, filling his trousers and underpants with sawdust! Other mischievous things went on, such as putting horrible smelling things into the hot glue pot on a gas ring burner. On one occasion a boy was allowed to make a chicken coop, which was so large that he could not get it through the door when it was finished.

The 'brains' in my family was my sister Diane. She used to carry her books to school in a large heavy satchel, which she insists made one of her shoulders lower than the other. On looking into that satchel recently she found an old exercise book marked 'VT Maths'. Mr Watkins, who was also her form teacher, took this subject. He lived in Victoria Road and every day would cycle along Rotherstone past our house. If it was raining he would hold one hand on the handle bar and carry his umbrella with the other hand while cycling!

John Girvan

Music and Drama

I CAME TO DGS from South Wilts Grammar School in Salisbury, when my father was moved to the Wiltshire Fire Brigade headquarters in Potterne. I had an interview with Mr John, the Headmaster, a quiet and gentle man and I had few qualms as I approached the first day at Braeside. The building was quite different from that which I was used to, and the names of the rooms, such as 'the back bedroom', caused some amusement.

I had wanted to study Music at A level but the school could not offer this, so I had to have my Music lessons out of school and concentrate on English and French, and, for a short while, Pure and Applied Maths. What a disaster that was! So instead I took pottery lessons with Mr Lynch. I found I really enjoyed that and succeeded in making quite an impressive coil pot – I wonder what happened to it?

At school in Salisbury I had always been very keen on drama and had taken part in many productions, on two noted occasions playing the male lead! Things were now to change as there were real males at Devizes and I was in two of Mr Haycock's highly esteemed productions, on the second occasion as a nun! I remember well the excitement of rehearsing, often quite late into the evening, and the *camaraderie* that built up among cast and crew.

The winning girls' choir in the Wiltshire Music Festival, May 1962

Music was my other real love. I was in choirs run by Mr Howells and taking part in the Wiltshire Music festival was the highlight of the year. As a very young girl I had travelled to the Festival from Salisbury with my village junior school – quite an adventure in those days. The carol party at Christmas, held in the canteen, was always keenly anticipated and well rehearsed. The singing of the Boar's Head carol as we trouped into B6 for refreshments is an enduring memory. The canteen was also the venue for Film Society, which opened my eyes to cinema that I would otherwise have overlooked.

At one stage, the VI form had lessons with a young teacher called Peter Brookes (who later followed an acting career and was in the late-lamented TV series 'Crossroads'). He was somewhat critical of us for not showing our individuality, so on one famous occasion we dressed up outrageously for one of his lessons. I remember wearing a huge green sweater, with a very short skirt and scarlet stockings.

French play-reading at Mr John's house was a completely new experience for me and I'm sure he and Miss Thomas would have been amazed to hear that, while teaching at a special school, I undertook the teaching of French and organised several trips to Cherbourg.

Sport was not my strong suit, but I did play some netball and tennis and was one of the team who provided the famous cricket teas during the summer fixtures – so many sandwiches! I really loved the Friday night dancing club and thought nothing of walking from the other end of town each week. What memories of the Eightsome Reel and the Mississippi Dip!

All in all, my memories of DGS are very happy ones and I remain friends with many of my fellow pupils. I should also mention that I met my husband there and we recently celebrated forty years of marriage, together with our two sons and our grandsons. Yes, DGS, you have a lot to answer for!

Jean Hancock (née Ware 1958-1960)

1,000 Lines!

ON WEDNESDAYS, the lesson immediately after morning break was History taught by Peter Daines. Most Wednesdays we were in the classroom before Mr Daines and spent the time chatting before he arrived. One day I noticed that the satchel of the girl sitting in front of me contained a tube of talcum powder. I gently removed the tube, shook it and gingerly twisted the lid. As I bounced the tube along the desk, a series of little puffs of powder shot out from the holes in the lid, resembling the smoke from a railway engine. The boy next to me, thinking that I was about to squirt him with talc, grabbed my hand. The resulting pressure on the tube caused a beautiful plume of powder to erupt across the back two rows of tables. Everyone thus sprayed immediately began to wipe the powder from their clothes and rub it from the surface of the tables. Mr Daines then entered and began his lesson. After a few moments he sniffed once or twice and then demanded, 'What's been going on in here?' adding, 'The place smells like a pigsty.'

Nobody spoke and Mr Daines became more insistent, making the sort of threats about loss of breaks and dinner-times that teachers often do in these circumstances. Finally, in a very small voice, I owned up and explained what had happened. I was not prepared for Mr Daines's reaction. 'One thousand lines, Henley— "I must leave other people's property alone".' By the end of the lesson he had commuted my sentence to seven hundred lines: one hundred on each of the following two days and one hundred on each day of the following week, to be delivered to the staff room during each morning break. At the end of the lesson, one of the girls in the class smiled at me and said, 'You were very brave to own up like that.' When you're only fourteen, that means a lot!

That evening, after doing my homework, I completed my hundred lines and then delivered them the following day. On the Thursday I wrote another hundred and handed those in on the Friday. During the weekend I decided to get ahead of Mr Daines's demands and wrote three hundred lines. On Monday I delivered the hundred due that day and was told by Mr Daines that he had been talking to other teachers and it seemed that I wasn't as daft as I looked. He then muttered, 'You can forget the rest of those lines, Henley.'

Years later, after qualifying as a teacher I was appointed to a post at St Peter's School. At one of several meetings between the staff of Devizes School and of the local primary schools I was one of the first to arrive at the seminar on 'Discipline in the classroom'. Soon after I arrived, Peter Daines came in, greeted me and then took the seat next to mine. I still regret not mentioning the thousand lines and the strange chance that had brought us together again.

I remember the ability of Mr Lewis, known as 'Lump', to draw a perfect circle, freehand, on the blackboard. One day, when I was in the sixth form, he failed and the circle he had just drawn had a distinct bulge on one side. He stood back from the board, looked at the circle and remarked, "That doesn't look quite right. It's got a lump on it." As we all stifled laughs, he turned to face us with a look of innocence on his face.

During the summer holidays following my appointment as a prefect, we decided to 'modernize' the Prefects' Lodge. We had been given a Belfast sink to replace the little basin in the kitchen, but had no means of attaching it to the wall under the single, cold tap. Someone acquired some bricks, sand and cement and I built a wall to support the sink. As it was the first wall I had built, I found that it was soon coming out to meet me and had to build the last couple of courses leaning inwards to compensate.

As a means of livening up free periods, when we were meant to be working, one of the prefects devised the 'Benger Dash'. Opposite Braeside was Bengers' sweet shop, run by Mrs Benger and her daughter, Heather. The 'Dash' involved the 'dasher' sitting in the chair next to the fireplace with the front door closed. Someone else would then look up and down the drive to make sure that no teacher was in sight and then time how long it took for the 'dasher' to go over to Bengers' shop, spend at least sixpence on sweets and return to the chair, having closed the front door.

Most of the teachers had nicknames. Mr Williams was 'Nana', Mr Bevan – 'Boo-Boo', Mr Dexter – 'Ted', Mr Lynch – 'Leonardo da Lynchi' and Miss Stevenson was 'Rocket'.

Chris Henley (1960-67)

A trip to remember

RETURNING TO LIVE in Wiltshire was always our intention, but we had imagined it to be part of our retirement years. Michael working for Swindon Borough Council during this last year is a most unexpected development.

An internal email from David Haycock to Michael, letting us know that a book of anecdotes was being compiled by his mother Lorna to celebrate 100 years of Devizes Grammar School was especially poignant. It was a school trip organised by the English teacher, Mr Haycock, to see *Henry V* some forty years ago that started our romantic involvement. School trips such as these were designed to broaden the mind and this one truly did. I don't expect for one moment David Haycock dreamt of the connection he was making between us all when he sent his email.

Michael and I both joined the Grammar School as rejects of the selection system. Michael had been at Gillingham Technical School where he was wasting away and I was plucked from Shurnhold Secondary Modern School by a vigilant Head. Mr Davis ('Zorro'!), the Devizes Grammar School Head, opened doors to a very different world. A strict but kind and generous man, he took a personal interest in us all. It was after the trip to *Henry V* that I noticed how fond he was of Michael, who was frequently allowed to stand outside his office.

We were of course part of the 'swinging sixties', when *Far from the Madding Crowd* came to town and the excitement of bumping into Julie Christie and Alan Bates in the Market Place Pie Shop was a real possibility It was a time when a number one haircut by one of the older boys sent girls into an hysterical frenzy; he was of course sent home. We can't imagine what it would take to have the same reaction today. It was also the time when DGS pupils were released from lessons to help to clean up the very neglected canal, which is now so well cared for and used.

What did the Grammar School do for us? For me it was like releasing a battery hen into a warm and friendly farmyard, free to wander and explore. Children played on rolling lawns surrounded by flower beds instead of a municipal-type playing field bounded by hedges and fences. We were freed from the enclosure of rectangular purpose-built rooms in the 1950s/1960s modern style, with its plastic floors and reinforced glass windows, into what felt like a very large family with a real sense of belonging. For Michael the icing on the cake, (and to the amazement of himself and his mates), was that he passed his English Literature exam, one of Mr Haycock's finest achievements.

Having experienced the other side, we have never taken for granted the opportunities given to us by Devizes Grammar School.

Michael Pitt (1962-1967); Maria Pitt (née Di Claudio 1965-1968)

School dinners and noxious gases

WE ALL LOOKED FORWARD to school dinners in those days. Nobody took a packed lunch as the meals were so good and cheap. If you were from a big family you got free meals. There were about ten large tables and the teachers sat above us on the stage. Each table of younger pupils had a sixth former with them to keep order and make sure everyone had a fair share. One person would collect a giant cottage pie or steak and kidney pie from the hatch. Another person would collect the big dish of vegetables and it would be shared out at the table, just like a family meal. The puddings, such as fruit crumble and custard, were wholesome.

We had swimming lessons with Sid Dowse at the swimming pool in Colston Road, where there was a large fountain and tiers of concrete seats. There was intense inter-house rivalry at the summer swimming sports and we also had tennis tournaments on the lawn at Braeside.

To an eleven year old, prefects seemed very grown up and glamorous. They wore a different tie and an enamel badge. Unfortunately I was never a prefect as the school went comprehensive in 1969 when I was fifteen and there were no prefects at the new school.

In the main building in Bath Road we had wooden desks, covered in graffiti. We had to make up ink from powder to fill the inkwells and we used ink pens and blotting paper. There were horrible smells from the Chemistry and Biology labs. The art room was a wooden hut presided over by Mr Lynch; we girls thought he was very handsome.

I remember Mr Haycock's production of *A Midsummer Night's Dream* in 1967. He hired the costumes from the Royal Shakespeare Company and they were really good. On the week of the play the girl playing Puck was taken ill, so Mr Haycock had to find a costume and take over the part at short notice, which called for a lot of agility and running around.

Barbara George (née Jessett 1964-1969)

A parent's perspective

I WAS NOT A PUPIL at DGS but my daughters were and I had private tuition from three of its teachers in 1938 to push me towards an Oxford School Certificate. In the last five years of the school I was Honorary Secretary of the Parent-Teachers Association. I was fortunate to know personally some delightful members of staff, the Classics master Haydn Howells, Maths teacher Harold Lewis, French master 'Froggy' Lund and Biology master Dickie Moore. I heard tales of other members of staff from my daughters – one who stood a pupil in a waste basket, another who arranged students in alphabetical order in the class room because it was easier then to remember their names. Of course all schools have their low as well as their high points. At one time in the early 1940s the married headmaster was pursuing a female member of staff and an unfortunate male teacher landed himself in prison for his interest in boys. One Empire Day on 24 May, the headmaster failed to put the Union Jack up the flagpole and Fred Chivers, head of the building firm of W.E.Chivers, threatened to hoist him on it!

All new pupils at the school and their parents were given a pep. talk, which often lasted an hour, by the Headmaster Tom Davis., in the main school. The only thing I remember learning was that girl pupils should not wear anything, not even confirmation crosses, round their necks, which, dangling, might interfere with their writing. School uniform was strictly observed. Miss Broadway made girls kneel on the floor while she went round with a tape measure, checking the distance from the floor to the hem of the skirt. One headmaster would stand at the foot of the staircase watching the girls as they came down, to check that their petticoats were regulation white, not red, as one girl found to her cost.

The annual Christmas carol concert was a highlight of the year. Some of the boys made a point of singing a familiar line thus – 'Hang the Polly (holly) in the hall'. This was annually anticipated with relish.

I took over as PTA Secretary in 1965, succeeding John Spencer. My last years as secretary were concerned with the long, futile and often acrimonious battle to keep the Grammar School in being. When the fight to save the Grammar School was over, Roy Kemp, Chairman of the Governors, told me he would have continued the fight but for his fear that in the interim a pupil might have met with an accident while crossing the double road to Braeside. This was an accident waiting to happen; fortunately it never did.

On the thirtieth anniversary of the outbreak of the Second World War, the comprehensive school opened on 3 September 1969. Tom Davis, Headmaster of DGS, became the first Head. He tried to run it on old grammar school lines and within weeks had sent a boy home with instructions to get his hair cut. But times had changed. The boy's mother contacted the *Gazette* and the boy's photograph ended up on the front page, alongside a column of mine on sheep-shearing!

John Leach

From Braeside and Back in Forty Five Years

HOW MANY OF US at sixteen years of age seriously think what we might be doing in forty-five years time? One thing is for sure – I could never imagine being back at Braeside.

My short time at DGS was a very happy time, although I don't think I realised it then. The teachers were slightly scary, some were very strict, some were kind and funny, others a mixture. After leaving school I went into administrative work, got married and had two lovely children. When the time came to return to work again, I became a secretary at the comprehensive school. Those scary, funny teachers became my colleagues. Years earlier they were 'Miss' or 'Sir'; now they were Bert, Lorna, Martin, Ron, Daphne etc. It was strange at first but in time those names slipped easily off my tongue. It soon became apparent that they weren't so scary after all and, despite what we might have thought of them, they were normal people!

When my marriage broke up and I had to find a full-time job, a colleague saw an advertisement for a secretary at Braeside, now a residential education centre. It is now twenty years since I came back to work at Braeside and how it has changed! The library is now the office, all the ground floor rooms are conference rooms, and the first and second floor rooms are bedrooms. I can walk into the former Headmaster's room, now 'Willow', and dream about what would have gone on there all those years ago. Just across the landing the former staff room now has bunk beds, with lots of small children sleeping soundly – well, sometimes! The top floor of the house, which in our day was out of bounds as it was the home of the caretaker, now sleeps twenty students. The old canteen met with a sad end when a beech tree fell across it during a heavy storm. We now have a smart, brick-built dining room, with carpet and curtains. Prior to the canteen's demise, the stage had been removed to make way for more tables.

The open-air theatre is no more. In its place is a pond where students dip for bugs. Gone are the lazy days of watching tennis being played on the top lawn; now on sunny days children can be seen playing volleyball. A sad thing was the demolition of the prefects' lodge some years ago. It was decided by the powers-that-be at County Hall that it wasn't cost effective to repair it.

A few years ago I met up with another old pupil and we are now married. He still enjoys coming to see me at the old school. Most years we have a handful of past pupils coming to Braeside, bringing their spouses, children and friends, asking if they can look round. It is always a pleasure to go round with them and reminisce about our school days. Without exception they all say it was a wonderful place and weren't we lucky to have been at school in such lovely surroundings. I feel so privileged to be still at Braeside and enjoy being 'back at school'.

Paulette Bremner-Milne (née Dicker, 1957-9)

The Tuck Shop

IN 1930 MY FAMILY opened a sweet shop. My uncle was very sceptical – he said we might as well sell winkles! The first day's takings amounted to 2s.6d., but things soon improved, especially when my mother started to make home-made ice cream. The children were sometimes given spoons to eat ice cream off the machine before it was washed. Ice cream finished during the Second World War. A student later reminisced that he had once eaten seventeen, which he could have done with while he was serving in India! When sweets came off ration, we could see that our supply was not going to go round, so we reduced the quantity, first to sixpence worth, then threepenny worth and finally a pennyworth. One day some boys came into the shop mid-morning for a smoke, when horror of horrors, who should be walking across the road but Mr Howells.

The approach to the school by the Nursery

The boys crouched down behind the counter. Mr Howells bought a packet of cigarettes and left, but the lads had learnt their lesson and never tried it again. Sometimes they would shake up a bottle of lemonade and as a result it would spurt all over the floor, but they were made to wipe it up. For the cross-country, the boys bought barley sugar for energy. When the school doctor had paid a visit, one of the boys said, 'Mrs Benger, I know where babies come from and I'm going to tell you', and he did!

Pranks often caused amusement. Once a teacher looked up to see a pair of legs dangling outside the classroom window. He raced upstairs, only to find a pair of stuffed stockings with shoes attached. On another occasion a boy pressed the emergency bell in the telephone kiosk and ran up the bank to watch the police car arrive. Someone once pulled the door knocker off the shop and was chased up the road. End of term antics included putting a potato in a teacher's car exhaust and putting a dustbin in a car. When we put up Christmas decorations in the shop, someone tried to knock down the balloons, but a good yell from Mother soon put an end to that!

But there was a good relationship between us and the pupils and between the staff and pupils. On Open Days children would often bring their parents over to the shop to be introduced. The prefects called in one day, saying that they were trying to decorate the lodge, but didn't have any wallpaper. Mother gave them two spare rolls and later they invited her over to see their handiwork. Mr Burt was very kind. Sometimes a tool that had been replaced found its way to a lad who didn't have much pocket money, When some boys had helped by bringing chairs back from the Corn Exchange, he treated them to an ice cream and had one himself. He said it was his only pleasure, as he had diabetes. The children, too, could be kind to each other. Once a group of girls came in and introduced us to a new girl – the she was the smallest we had ever seen. We measured her against the counter and she was only just level. The others formed a protective guard around her.

In 1967 the day came when the room was needed and the shop had to close. We closed it quickly so as not to upset the children. They had asked if anything could be done to carry it on. But two years later the school itself closed and the Grammar School was no more.

The school was like a second home to the students. They often were mischievous but meant no harm. The school was not so large as to stifle individuality and it was a happy school.

Heather Benger

Construction beneath the stage 1945

A proper stage at last

Lady Windermere's Fan

Drama

PERHAPS THE MOST VALUABLE legacy from school days is not what is learnt in class, but what interests are awakened by out of school activities. Many of the previous contributors have written of their love of sport, music and drama, which had been kindled at school. Drama particularly develops poise and confidence, is a good social mixer and team building exercise. Over the years drama at DGS developed into a strong and very successful part of the life of the school.

Pre-war drama featured one act plays or scenes from longer plays, sometimes in co-operation with old students, Performances were given in the Bath Road building with the temporary stage propped up with Latin books, or sometimes in the Cheese Hall in town. In the summer of 1945, when the kitchen and dining hall were built, the opportunity was taken to construct a stage raised on three low brick walls, funded from the proceeds of the summer fête. The acting area was famously tiny – fifteen feet by ten feet, with an opening seven feet high because of the slope of the roof, which had an angle of 23 degrees, so all stage flats had to cut at that angle. Staff and pupils worked on the construction, with wiring underneath for lighting, which was assembled in the school lab. A sturdy iron framework, personally tested by Mr Burt, supported the scenery and curtain rail.

With a permanent area now for acting, the choice of plays became more ambitious. Performances of costume plays such as 'Berkeley Square'. 'Lady Windermere's Fan' and 'Pygmalion' followed under the guidance of Dick Scruton. His successor, Bert Haycock arrived in 1952, and those who were involved in any way with the plays will recollect his high standards and inspired talent as a producer, with the ability to draw out creditable performances from inexperienced actors as well as gifted individuals. He was ably supported as Stage Manager by Ron Beasley, who assembled and trained enthusiastic stage crews, with technical help in making and painting scenery from the Art and Woodwork departments. The wardrobe was run by myself and a succession of keen senior girl assistants.

In 1953 a new dimension was added to dramatic performances by the construction of the open-air theatre in the grounds of Braeside. This was the

Opening of the open air theatre on 2 July 1953 by Alderman W E Stevens, Chairman of Wiltshire County Council Education Committee, accompanied by C W Pugh, Chairman of the Governors, and the Headmaster

brain-child of Headmaster Denys John and commemorated the coronation of Queen Elizabeth II. The theatre was designed on the lines of a Greek classical theatre, with a semi-circular stage, thirty feet in diameter, raised two feet at the front and five feet at the back and an arena twenty feet in diameter accessible from the stage by two wooden and brick stairways. A hedge was planted at the back of the stage, with ten cypress trees on one side and two others in tubs each side. Two-tier seating was provided for an audience of 150 and the whole area was planted with Bromham turf. Plans were drawn up by the Fifth Form Technical Drawing class and the theatre was constructed by the Braeside gardeners Mr Gingell and Mr Bowden. The total cost was £25. The theatre was opened on 2 July 1953 by Alderman W.E.Stevens, Chairman of the Wiltshire Education Committee, and a commemorative tablet was sunk in the arena. Sadly, the theatre has now been converted into a pond for visiting students to Braeside.

The theatre provided a splendid setting for the performance of *Merrie England* in 1953 by a cast of pupils, staff and old students. So popular was it that an extra matinée had to be put on. The following year *The Mikado* was performed, with the addition of a willow pattern bridge, ingeniously designed and built by Ron Beasley. Several members of staff took leading roles – Dick Moore in the

Merrie England, 1953

Merrie England, 1953

Merrie England, 1953

The Mikado, 1954

title role, Haydn Howells as Nanki-Poo, Bert Haycock as Ko-Ko and Margaret Davies as Katisha. The make up for this production was quite a challenge, and though the principals' costumes were hired, parents and the wardrobe girls made a splendid job of sewing and embroidering the chorus costumes.

Thirteen years later came perhaps the most memorable open-air production – *A Midsummer Night's Dream*, for which the setting was magical. This was produced by intensive rehearsals with a group of post-exam students over a period of three weeks. Fortunately this was one of the most experienced and talented group of actors and the performances were over-subscribed. One member of the audience wrote, ' The magnificent natural setting at Braeside coupled with the splendid costumes

The Mikado, 1954

Midsummer Night's Dream , 1967

Midsummer Night's Dream , 1967

helped to lift it into a class of its own'. A visitor from America was equally enchanted, writing in August 1967, 'I will never forget that absolutely beautiful and moving (and *funny*) Midsummer Night's Dream done by your Grammar School in the 1960s on the back lawn under the stars—it was **excellent**' So agreed the judges for the Wiltshire Drama Association Award for the best production in the county in competition with adult groups.

The following year, *Twelfth Night*, using many of the *Midsummer Night's Dream* cast, was performed to acclaim, but sadly was the last of the major open-air productions. Meanwhile, highly successful and entertaining Christmas plays had been performed on the minute dining hall stage, two winning the coveted county drama awards – *Dandy Dick* in 1957 and *The Matchmaker* in 1963. *Dandy Dick*, a Pinero farce, involved hasty backstage costume and scenery changes, achieved with swift precision by actors and stage crew alike. *Ring Round the Moon* in 1966 even featured a wheelchair on that tiny stage.

The Enchanted in 1968 was a particularly poignant production, the last of the Grammar School series. A reception was held after the last night for cast, stage crew, wardrobe girls, and former actors and supporters. An engraved silver salver was presented to Bert Haycock, bearing the simple message 'Thank you', which I know touched him greatly.

Lorna Haycock (née Read 1951-1959)

Twelfth Night, 1968

Dramatic Society Productions

1936.	She Stoops to Conquer
1937-8	One Act Plays
	Four plays by staff, pupils and old students
	Four plays by pupils and old students
1944	Distinguished Gathering
	One Act Plays
1945	Dangerous Company
1946	I Have Five Daughters
1947	Wives and Daughters
1948	Berkeley Square
1949	Lady Windermere's fan
1950	Dear Brutus
1951	Pygmalion
1952	Thunder Rock
1953	Merrie England; The Prodigious Snob
1954	The Mikado; Arms and the Man
1955	The Snow Queen
1956	The Women have their Way; The Play of the Weather
1957	Dandy Dick
1958	Lady Precious Stream
1959	Cradle Song
1960	—-
1961	Jonah and the Whale
1962	Sganarelle; Antigone
1963	The Matchmaker
1964	The Magistrate
1965	The Bald Prima Donna; Barnstable; Out of the Flying Pan
1966	Ring Round the Moon
1967	Midsummer Night's Dream; Doctor's Delight
1968	Twelfth Night; The Enchanted

Thunder Rock, 1952

The Prodigious Snob, 1952

The Prodigious Snob, 1952

Arms and the Man, 1954

The Snow Queen, 1955

The Snow Queen, 1955

DEVIZES GRAMMAR SCHOOL 1906 – 1969 133

The Women have their Way, 1956

Lady Precious Stream, 1958

Antigone, 1962

The Matchmaker, 1963

Ring round the Moon, 1966

Epilogue

WHAT, THEN, was the secret of this school? What made it so special that still old pupils meet regularly in formal and informal reunions? It certainly was not the facilities, equipment or space. The division into two buildings either side of a busy main road and the increasingly cramped conditions made school life difficult. But in some ways, the nurturing of the junior school in more formal surroundings established a discipline to support the greater informality enjoyed by pupils at Braeside, with its delightful grounds, woods and family atmosphere. The ethos of the school was created by the differing contributions of the five headmasters and the long and dedicated service of firm but caring staff, who established a good relationship with pupils. The size of the school, too, helped to foster a sense of community and *camaraderie*. Pupils of different abilities and backgrounds participated in a myriad of extra-curricular activities, which often created life-long friendships and interests. And that is what education should do- establish a firm basis for future development and careers, but also to awaken curiosity, create confidence and develop the talents and abilities of the individual child. In its sixty-three year history, DGS has produced some fine, charming and well-rounded men and women; that must be its epitaph.

Reunion of the Class of '29, in 1996

Reunion at Worton, 2005. Left to right: Tony Duck, David Ponting, Tony Coleman, Shelagh Newland, David Brown, Mary Ellis, Stephanie Offer, Pauline Bradbury, Roger Swift, Lorna Haycock, Jill Lawes, Keith Wiltshire, Valerie Hambleton, Peter Lawes, Pauline Newland

Class of '47 reunion at Braeside, May 2006